W9-DAI-743

Microsoft
FrontPage 2000
At a Glance

Microsoft Press

PUBLISHED BY
Microsoft Press
A Division of Microsoft Corporation
One Microsoft Way
Redmond, Washington 98052-6399

Library of Congress Cataloging-in-Publication Data
Nelson, Stephen L., 1959-
    Microsoft FrontPage 2000 At a Glance / Stephen L. Nelson.
        p. cm.
    Includes index.
    ISBN 1-57231-951-8
    1. Microsoft FrontPage.   2. Web sites--Design.   3. Web publishing.
    I. Title.
    TK5105.8885.M53N45   1999
    005.7'2--dc21   98-43586
                                                           CIP

Printed and bound in the United States of America.

1 2 3 4 5 6 7 8 9   WCWC   4 3 2 1 0 9

Distributed in Canada by ITP Nelson, a division of Thomson Canada Limited.

A CIP catalogue record for this book is available from the British Library.

Microsoft Press books are available through booksellers and distributors worldwide. For further information about international editions, contact your local Microsoft Corporation office or contact Microsoft Press International directly at fax (425) 936-7329. Visit our Web site at mspress.microsoft.com.

For Stephen L. Nelson, Inc.
Writers: Jason Gerend and Steve Nelson
Project Editor: Paula Thurman
Technical Editor: Brian Milbrath

For Microsoft Press
Acquisitions Editor: Susanne M. Forderer
Project Editor: Laura Sackerman

Contents

"How do I add a folder to a web?"

See page 9

Check up on the state of your web site.
See page 23

Create a style sheet to unify the look of your web site.
See page 58

"How do I specify text wrapping?"

See page 68

*"How do I change
the look of a
table's borders?"*

See page 112

Add a new page to a frame.
See page 122

Monitor web site traffic.
See page 132

"How do I create a user registration page?"

See page 155

*"How do I make
information in
a database
accessible to web
site visitors?"*

See page 180

Check out a file so that other
users cannot edit it at the
same time you do.
See page 200

10 Administering a Web Site 183

Index 205

1

About This Book

Microsoft *FrontPage 2000 At a Glance* is for anyone who wants to begin web publishing with Microsoft FrontPage 2000. I think you'll find this book to be a straightforward, easy-to-read, and easy-to-use reference tool. With the premise that web publishing isn't something only the experts can (or should) do, this book's purpose is to help you get your work done quickly and efficiently so that you can focus your efforts on the most important and more enjoyable parts of web publishing: finding, packaging, and presenting interesting or useful information.

No Computerese!

Let's face it—when there's a task you don't know how to do but you need to get it done in a hurry, or when you're stuck in the middle of a task and can't figure out what to do next, there's nothing more frustrating than having to read page after page of technical background material. You want the information you need—nothing more, nothing less—and you want it now! And the information should be easy to find and understand.

That's what this book is all about. It's written in plain English—no technical jargon and no computerese. There's no single task in the book that takes more than two pages. Just look up the task in the index or the table of contents, turn to the page, and there it is. Each task introduction gives you information that is essential to performing the task, suggesting situations in which you can use the task or providing examples of the benefit you gain from completing the procedure. The task itself is laid out step by step and accompanied by a graphics image that adds visual clarity. Just read the introduction, follow the steps, look at the illustrations, and get your work done with a minimum of hassle.

You may want to turn to another task if the one you're working on has a "See Also" in the left column. Because there's a lot of overlap among tasks, I didn't want to keep repeating myself; you might find more elementary or more advanced tasks laid out on the pages referenced. I've also added some useful tips here and there and offered a "Try This" once in a while to give you a context in which to use the task. But, by and large, I've tried to remain true to the heart and soul of the book, which is that the information you need should be available to you *at a glance*.

What's New

If you're looking for what's new in FrontPage 2000, just look for this new icon **New**2000 inserted throughout the book. You will find the new icon in the table of contents so you can quickly and easily identify new or improved features in FrontPage. You will also find the new icon on the first page of each section. There it will serve as a handy reminder of the latest improvements in FrontPage as you move from one task to another.

Useful Tasks...

Whether you use FrontPage 2000 for web publishing on the Internet or an intranet, I've tried to pack this book with procedures for everything I could think of that you might want to do, from the simplest tasks to some of the more esoteric ones.

...And the Easiest Way To Do Them

Another thing I've tried to do in *Microsoft FrontPage 2000 At a Glance* is to find and document the easiest way to accomplish a task. FrontPage 2000 often provides many ways to obtain a single result, which can be daunting or delightful, depending on the way you like to work. If you tend to stick with one favorite and familiar approach, the methods described in this book are the way to go. If you prefer to try out alternative techniques, go ahead! The intuitiveness of FrontPage invites exploration, and you're likely to discover ways of doing things that you think are easier or that you like better. If you do, that's great! It's exactly what the creators of FrontPage had in mind when they provided so many alternatives.

A Quick Overview

You don't have to read this book in any particular order. The book is designed so that you can jump in, get the information you need, and then close the book, keeping it near your computer until the next time you need it. But that doesn't mean I scattered the information about with wild abandon. If you were to read the book from front to back, you'd find a logical progression from the simple tasks to the more complex ones. Here's a quick overview.

First, I assume that FrontPage 2000 is already installed on your machine. If it's not, the Setup Wizard makes installation so simple that you won't need my help anyway. So, unlike most computer books, this one doesn't start out with installation instructions and a list of system requirements. You've already got that under control.

Section 2 tells you the basics of how to use FrontPage to work with a web site.

Section 3 explains how you create and add text and hyperlinks to your web pages.

Section 4 explains how to incorporate graphic content into your web pages. It describes how you place graphic images and work with them using FrontPage.

Section 5 goes into more detail on working with web pages. It guides you through positioning objects on your web page, adding color schemes to your pages, applying advanced animation effects to your text and images, and other advanced tasks.

The remaining five sections of this book delve into more advanced web publishing topics: Section 6, for example, explains how you add tables to your web pages, and Section 7 explains how you work with frames. Section 8 tells you how to use FrontPage Components in your web site, and Section 9 explains how you use forms. and Section 10 describes how you administer a web site.

A Final Word (or Two)

I had three goals in writing this book. I want this book to help you:

- ◆ Do all the things you want to do with FrontPage 2000.
- ◆ Discover how to do things you didn't know you wanted to do with FrontPage.
- ◆ Enjoy your web publishing work with FrontPage.

My "thank you" for buying this book is the achievement of those goals. I hope you'll have as much fun using *Microsoft FrontPage 2000 At a Glance* as I've had writing it. The best way to learn is by doing, and that's what I hope you'll get from this book.

Jump right in!

2

The Basics of FrontPage

Microsoft FrontPage helps you create and administer web sites. This section describes how you use FrontPage to create and work with web sites, or "webs" as FrontPage calls them. The following sections provide step-by-step instructions for creating the web page documents that make up a web site. If the terms *web site* and *web page* are unfamiliar to you, read the "What Is a World Wide Web Site?" sidebar on page 7. It provides useful background information on the World Wide Web.

This section is designed to help you get comfortable working with web sites in FrontPage. Although FrontPage can work with web pages independent of a web site, FrontPage offers so many powerful web-site administration tools that it's preferable to manage your whole web site with FrontPage rather than using it just to edit individual web pages.

If you have trouble finding a menu command or toolbar button that is described in the text, it could be because FrontPage has personalized your menus and toolbars by hiding infrequently used menu commands and toolbar buttons. To display hidden menu commands, click the down arrow at the bottom of a menu. To display hidden toolbar buttons, click the down arrow at the far right end of a toolbar and then click the toolbar button you want.

Opening a Web Site or Web Page

If you already have a web site (or web as FrontPage calls it) created, you need to open the web to begin working on it in FrontPage.

TIP

Webs vs. web sites. *In this book, I use the terms* web *and* web site *synonymously. To make a distinction between the two terms, however, a web site is called a web while it's in FrontPage, but after it's published to a web server, a web is known as a web site.*

TIP

Close a web or web page. *Choose Close or Close Web from the File menu to close the currently open web page or web.*

Open a Web or Web Page

1. Click the down arrow next to the Open toolbar button, and choose from the drop-down menu either Open Web to open a web site or Open to open a web page.

2. Select the folder in which your web or file is stored from the Look In drop-down list box or by using the shortcut icons on the Places Bar. To open a web page, select the file.

3. Click Open.

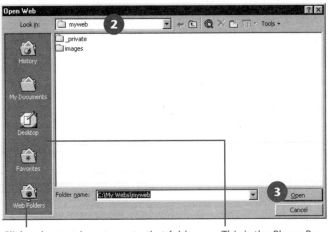

Click a shortcut icon to go to that folder.　　　This is the Places Bar.

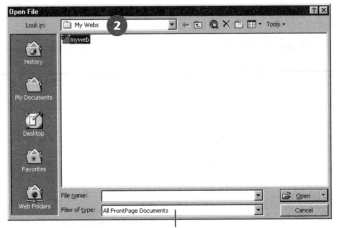

Choose which type of file you want to view here.

What Is a World Wide Web Site?

The World Wide Web (also known as W^3, the Web, and WWW) is just a set of multimedia documents that are connected by way of hyperlinks so that you can jump from one document to another, usually with a mouse click. If this definition sounds complicated, it's probably because it includes a handful of terms you might not know: documents, multimedia, and hyperlinks. Let me define these terms for you and clear up the picture.

Let's start with the key term, *document*. A document is just a report that describes something. Often, documents are on paper. In fact, you've probably created hundreds of paper documents: book reports in grade school; thank-you letters to distant, gift-giving relatives; and perhaps lengthy term papers in college. You wrote these documents on paper, but if you had produced and displayed them on a computer screen, they still would have been documents.

The *multimedia* part relates to the fact that when you create and display a document on a computer, you aren't limited to words. You can place pictures in a document, for example. And you can place sounds in documents as well. Just about any object a computer can create, display, or play can be placed in a document.

And now we come to what makes the World Wide Web unique—the *hyperlink* part. Hyperlinks are connections that let you jump from one document to another. Suppose, for example, that you're reading a document about the U.S. Department of Commerce and what it does. This document references, let's say, the Office of the President, with a hyperlink. You click on the words *Office of the President* and see a new document that talks about the president.

So to return to my original definition, the World Wide Web is simply a set of multimedia documents that are connected using hyperlinks. By clicking the hyperlinks, you can jump from one document to another.

To view a World Wide Web document, you need to have a web browser such as Microsoft Internet Explorer. The documents you read, or view, with a web browser are written using something called HTML code. In fact, the web browser uses HTML code to display a document on your screen. The HTML code also includes, in the case of the hyperlinks, uniform resource locators, or URLs, which describe the precise addresses of other HTML documents.

Creating a New Web Site

If you haven't already created the web site you want to work with in FrontPage, you need to do so first. While the notion of creating a conglomeration of linked pages might seem like a daunting task, FrontPage's wizards and templates make this step a simple one.

TIP

My Webs is the default directory. *By default, FrontPage stores the new webs you create in the My Webs directory on your computer. If you want to store a web somewhere else while you're working on it, you can enter another location on your hard drive or on the World Wide Web.*

TIP

Server extensions. *The Discussion Web and the Customer Support Web require that your web server have FrontPage Server Extensions installed in order to be fully functional.*

Create a New Web Site

1. Click the down arrow next to the New Page toolbar button, and choose Web from the drop-down menu.

2. Select the web template or wizard that best fits your new web.

3. Click OK to accept the default location for your web, or specify a different location in the Options drop-down list box.

4. If you selected a wizard, follow the instructions provided, and click Finish when you're done.

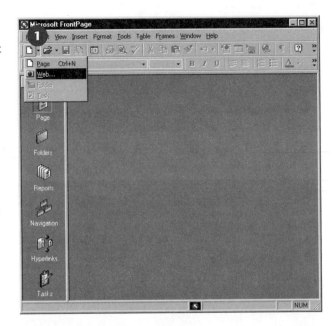

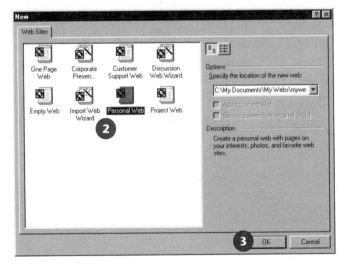

Creating New Pages and Folders

Adding new web pages and folders to your web site is a critical part of maintaining a web site. Fortunately, FrontPage makes it extremely easy to create single web pages or to add new folders and pages to an open web site.

TIP

Create a blank page. *To quickly create a blank web page, click the New Page toolbar button.*

Create a New Web Page

1. Click the Page button on the Views bar.

2. In the Page view, choose New from the File menu and then choose Page from the submenu.

3. Click either the General or Frames Pages tab, depending on whether you want to make a page containing frames.

4. Select a template from the list, and then click OK.

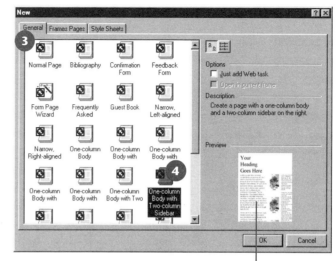

The currently selected template is previewed here.

Add a Folder to a Web

1. Open the web site to which you want to add a folder.

2. In the Folder List, right-click the folder in which you want to create a folder, and then choose New Folder from the shortcut menu.

3. Type a name for your folder, and then press the Enter key.

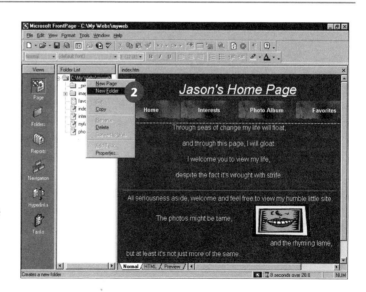

Using FrontPage Web Wizards

FrontPage's web wizards make it easy for you to create web sites. These wizards ask you a series of questions by using buttons and boxes in dialog boxes; you answer the questions by clicking the buttons and entering information in the boxes. If you've never used a wizard, you may want to read about what happens when you run one.

Describe the Web Pages You Want

The first dialog box displayed by a web wizard states that you've started a web wizard, and it alerts you that you'll be asked a series of questions about what you want your web site to look like. To continue, click Next. (While you're running the wizard, you can click Next to move ahead to the next web wizard dialog box or Back to go back to the previous web wizard dialog box.)

The real action begins with the second web wizard dialog box. It asks which pages you want to include by using a list of check boxes, as shown in the following figure. You choose which pages you want by selecting the appropriate check boxes. If you don't know whether you want a particular page or not, go ahead and accept the wizard's initial, or suggested, setting. If you decide later that you've made a mistake, it's easy to add or remove a page.

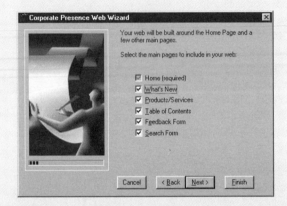

Explain How You Want Your Web Pages Organized

After you indicate which pages you want included in your web site, the wizard asks about—well, actually suggests—sections for the pages you've selected. In essence, by answering this set of questions, you partially describe how you want your web pages organized. For example, you'll be asked about what sections you want on your web site's home page. And you'll be asked about what sections you want on your What's New page.

Provide Any Standard Page Information

Once you've described the pages you want and how you want them organized, the wizard asks what information you want to include on each and every page. As elsewhere in the wizard's dialog boxes, you specify what you want the wizard to do by selecting check boxes.

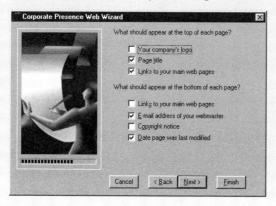

Pick a Look for Your Web Site

You also get to pick a look for your web site. Just click Choose Web Theme, and then select a theme for your web site. If you like one of the themes but don't want to have a background image, click the Background Picture check box to clear it. It's easy to change a web's theme later. (I describe how to do this in "Using Themes" on pages 87–88.)

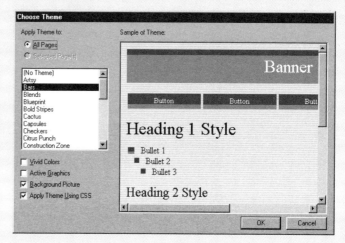

The FrontPage Window

Views bar

The Views bar provides buttons you click to switch between different views of your web site.

Page view

Page view lets you edit a web page while enabling you to drag files from your web into your current document.

Folder List

The Folder List shows you all the files and folders in your current web.

Normal tab

Use this tab for most or all of your web page creation and editing.

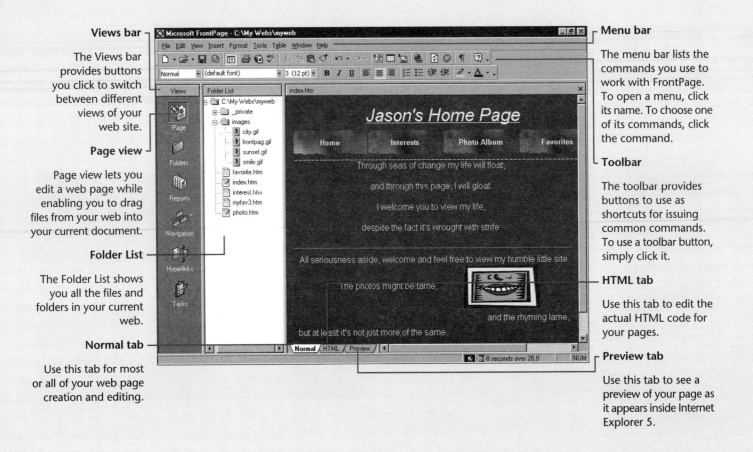

Menu bar

The menu bar lists the commands you use to work with FrontPage. To open a menu, click its name. To choose one of its commands, click the command.

Toolbar

The toolbar provides buttons to use as shortcuts for issuing common commands. To use a toolbar button, simply click it.

HTML tab

Use this tab to edit the actual HTML code for your pages.

Preview tab

Use this tab to see a preview of your page as it appears inside Internet Explorer 5.

Working with Folders and Page Views

After you've created a web site, FrontPage allows you to look at and examine the web site in several different ways. Folders and Page views list the web pages and images that make up your web site. Because these views resemble Windows Explorer, they are easy to work with.

TRY THIS

Change column width. *To change the width of a Folders view column, drag the right edge of the column heading button.*

TIP

Sort pages in Folders view. *Click a column heading button in Folders view to sort your web pages by that attribute.*

Work with Files in Folders or Page View

1. Open the web site you want to view.

2. Click the Page button on the Views bar.

3. To perform an action on a file, open the folder that contains the file in the Folder List and scroll to the file.

   ◆ Double-click a file to open it.

   ◆ Drag a file to a different folder to move it.

   ◆ Right-click a file, and choose Delete from the shortcut menu to delete the file.

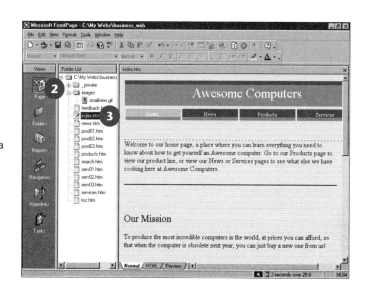

Working with Navigation View

Navigation view lets you view and construct an intuitive tree view of your web site, which FrontPage uses to determine which pages to link to on automatically generated navigation bars. As its name suggests, Navigation view is also an excellent tool for moving to different parts of your web site.

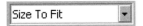

Size To Fit

TIP

Sized to fit. *If some of the files don't fit on the screen in Navigation view, click the Zoom button on the Navigation toolbar and select Size To Fit from the drop-down menu.*

Move Around on the Tree

1 Click the plus sign (+) on the web page that contains the hyperlinks you want to explore.

2 To collapse a portion of the Hyperlinks view map, click the minus sign (-) on a web page or image.

3 Click the background, and drag to move around in the view.

4 Click the Portrait/Landscape button on the Navigation toolbar to change the orientation of the tree view from top-down to left-right.

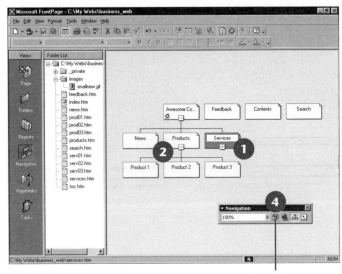

Click here to toggle between Portrait and Landscape views.

TIP

Specify pages to leave off navigation bars. *To tell FrontPage not to include a page on navigation bars it creates, toggle the Include In Navigation Bars button on the Navigation toolbar.*

Work with Pages in Navigation View

1 Open the web site you want to view.

2 Click the Navigation button on the Views bar.

3 Find the page you want. If you don't see it, click the minus sign to collapse a branch of the tree or click a plus sign to expand it.

◆ Double-click a page to open it.

◆ Drag a page to a different folder in the Folder List to move it.

◆ Right-click a page, and choose Delete from the shortcut menu to delete the file from Navigation view or the web site.

◆ Drag a page to a new location on the tree to change how FrontPage links to the page.

◆ To add a page to Navigation view, drag it from the Folder List to the Navigation tree.

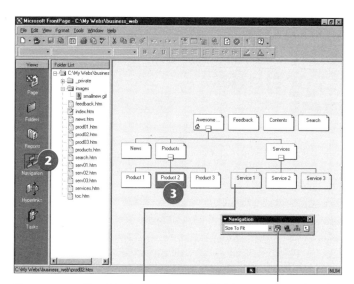

These pages will not be included on navigation bars.

Click here to rotate the view.

2

Working with Hyperlinks View

Hyperlinks view works almost the same as Navigation view, except that Hyperlinks view shows all hyperlinks to and from a page, not just the significant ones. Hyperlinks view can be useful in determining how visitors get to a particular page.

TRY THIS

Center a page. *Right-click the web page that you want to center, and then choose Move To Center from the shortcut menu.*

TIP

Switch to another page. *You can change the portion of the web site displayed in Hyperlinks view by clicking a different page of the web site in the Folders List.*

Work with Files in Hyperlinks View

1. Open the web site you want to view.

2. Click the Hyperlinks button on the Views bar.

3. To perform an action on a file, open the folder that contains the file in the Folder List and scroll to the file.

   ◆ Double-click a file to open it.

   ◆ Drag a file to a different folder to move it.

   ◆ Right-click a file, and choose Delete from the shortcut menu to delete the file.

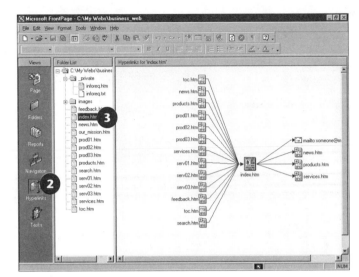

Viewing Web Pages

FrontPage provides three different document tabs for viewing open web pages: Normal, HTML, and Preview. These tabs make it easy to work with your web pages, while keeping the power of the source code close at hand.

TIP

Preview in browser. *Although the Preview tab displays your web page rendered through Internet Explorer, it is helpful to see how your web page looks when it is maximized in your browser. Click the Preview In Browser toolbar button to open your web page in your default web browser.*

TIP

View your home page. *To view your home page—the page that visitors see first when they browse to your web site—open the index.htm file.*

Use Different View Tabs

1️⃣ Open the web page you want by double-clicking it in any view.

2️⃣ Click a tab to see the web page in that view.

◆ Use the Normal tab to edit the web page as it appears in a web browser.

◆ Use the HTML tab to manually edit the source code for a page.

◆ Use the Preview tab to see how the page looks in Internet Explorer.

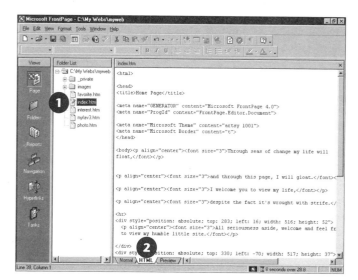

Removing and Renaming Files

You use FrontPage not only to create and edit web pages but also to manage files in your web site. When you use FrontPage for your file management, FrontPage helps you keep your web site free of broken links by automatically updating or removing links to files you rename or delete.

TIP

The Delete key. *You can quickly delete just about anything by selecting it and then pressing the Delete key on your keyboard.*

TIP

Don't delete your home page. *If you delete your home page, index.htm, and don't replace it with another index.htm, visitors won't be able to view any pages on your web site.*

Remove a Web Page or Image from the Web Site

1. Display your web site in Page, Folders, Navigation, or Hyperlinks view.

2. Right-click the web page or image you want to remove from the web site.

3. Choose the shortcut menu's Delete command.

4. When FrontPage asks you to confirm the delete, click Yes.

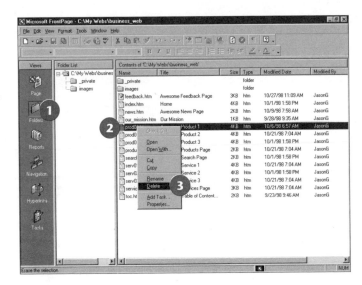

Rename a File

1. Click the file or folder you want to rename.

2. Wait a moment, and then click it again.

3. Edit the filename, being careful to leave the three-letter file extension unchanged.

4. Press the Enter key when you're finished.

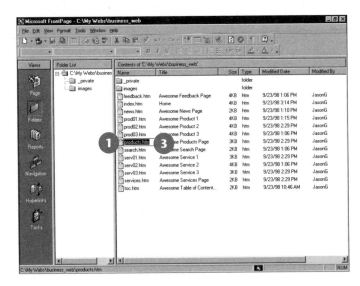

Moving and Copying Files

FrontPage makes file management very easy for you, especially when you have to move a file. If you used Windows Explorer to move a file in your web, all the pages that originally pointed to the file you moved would have broken links. If you use FrontPage to move your files, however, FrontPage automatically updates all the links to the file you move, saving you many broken links.

> **TIP**
>
> **Hard-to-drag places.** *If you can't drag the file to the folder you want, right-click the file, and choose Cut from the shortcut menu to move the file. (Or choose Copy to copy the file.) Then right-click the folder in which you want to place the file, and choose Paste from the shortcut menu.*

Move or Copy a File

1. Right-click the file in the Folder List you want to copy, and while holding down the right mouse button, drag the file to the folder in which you want to copy it.

2. Choose Copy Here from the shortcut menu to make a copy of the file in the new folder.

3. Choose Move Here from the shortcut menu to move the file to the new folder. FrontPage automatically updates any changed hyperlinks.

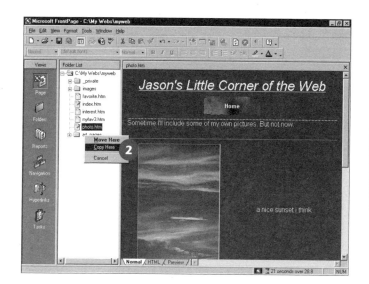

Importing Web Content

If you feel more comfortable working with another program, such as a word processing or image editing program, to create web content or edit existing content, you can easily do so. Then, after you have created the content, you can import it into FrontPage to prepare for publishing on the web.

TIP

Import a folder. *To import a folder, choose Import from the File menu. In the Import dialog box, click Add Folder, select the folder you want to import, and click OK. Click Close to import the folder and all of its files into your web.*

TIP

Import with no open web. *When you close all open web sites and choose Import from the File menu, FrontPage starts the Import Web Wizard, which guides you through creating a new web from a folder.*

Import a Web Page or Image

1. Open the web site where you want to place the new, imported web page or image.

2. Choose Import from the File menu.

3. Click Add File.

4. Find the folder containing the file you want to import in the Look In drop-down list box.

5. Select the file by double-clicking it.

6. Repeat steps 3, 4, and 5 to add more files to the list of pages to import.

7. Click OK to add the web pages and images to the open web site.

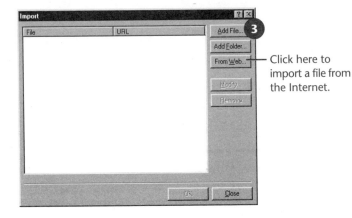

Click here to import a file from the Internet.

Saving and Exporting Web Pages

After you've created a web page, you need to save it. FrontPage integrates the saving process with the exporting process. Choose where you want to save your page, and FrontPage takes care of the rest.

TIP

Image files are bundled.
When you save a web page using the Save As command, all images and files necessary to display the web page properly are included with it, eliminating the need to export the image files separately.

Save or Export a Web Page

1. Open the web site to which you want to add a page or from which you want to export a page.

2. Select or create a web page.

3. Choose Save As from the File menu.

4. Specify the folder in which you want to save the web page or image in the Save In drop-down list box.

5. Type a name in the File Name text box, if necessary.

6. Click Save.

7. Specify which image files to save with the web page and where to save them.

8. Click OK.

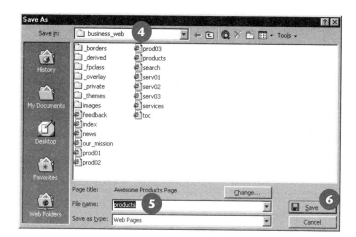

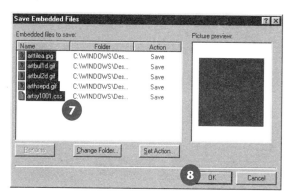

Finding and Replacing Text in a Web Site

Normally, you'll work with your web page text on a page-by-page basis, but FrontPage also lets you work with all your web pages at the same time. For example, you can easily find and replace text strings in all your web pages simultaneously.

Find and Replace Text in Your Web

1. Choose Find or Replace from the Edit menu to find a text fragment or to find and replace a text fragment.

2. Type the text you want to search for in the Find What text box.

3. If you chose the Replace command, type the text you want to substitute in the Replace With text box.

4. Select a Find Where option to search your entire web or only the current page, and then click either Find Next or Find In Web.

5. If you chose Find In Web, double-click a page in the list to view the text fragment in that page.

6. Click Replace to replace the text, or click Replace All to replace all occurrences of the text in the open page.

7. If you chose Find In Web, you can postpone viewing a page or replacing text by selecting the page and then clicking Add Task. FrontPage adds this task to your Tasks view.

8. Click Close when you're finished.

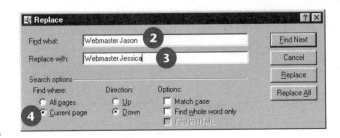

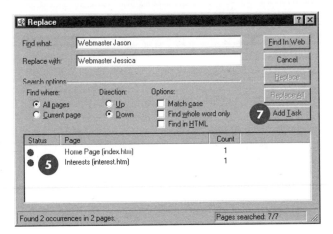

Viewing Reports on Your Web Site

The Reports view is the central repository for information about your web site and its pages and files. With Reports view you can find out just about anything you need to know concerning the state of your web: how many broken links you have, how many pages take too long to download, how much disk space your web site consumes, and much more.

TIP

Change report settings. *You can change the settings on the reports by choosing Options from the Tools menu, and then clicking the Reports View tab.*

Work with Reports View

1. Open the web whose information you want to view.

2. Click the Reports button on the Views bar.

3. Double-click an item in Reports view to see the list of files in question.

4. Click the Report toolbar button on the Reports toolbar and select Site Summary to return to the Site Summary report.

Click here to select a report.   Click here to verify hyperlinks.

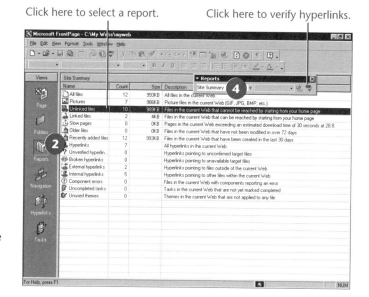

Checking Your Web Site's Hyperlinks

As you make changes to your web site (or as others make changes to it), you'll need to update, or refresh, your Hyperlinks view map regularly so that the map reflects reality. After you've added all your web pages and inserted hyperlinks where appropriate, you'll want to check that the links work correctly. FrontPage provides two tools you can use to perform this link-checking: the Verify Hyperlinks toolbar button in the Reports view and Re-calculate Hyperlinks on the Tools menu.

TIP

Stop verification. *Click the Stop toolbar button to stop the verification process.*

Verify Your Web Site's Hyperlinks

1 Open the web site you want to view.

2 Click the Reports button on the Views bar.

3 Click the Verify Hyperlinks toolbar button.

4 Select an option to tell FrontPage which hyperlinks to verify.

♦ Click the Verify All Hyperlinks option button to verify all broken or unknown hyperlinks.

♦ Click the Resume Verification option button if you previously started to verify hyperlinks but stopped before completing the verification.

♦ Click the Verify Selected Hyperlinks option button to verify only the hyperlinks you select (you must be viewing a hyperlink report).

5 Click Start. When FrontPage finishes verifying the hyperlinks, it displays the status of your hyperlinks in the Broken Hyperlinks report.

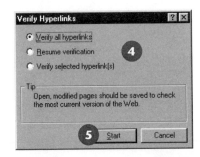

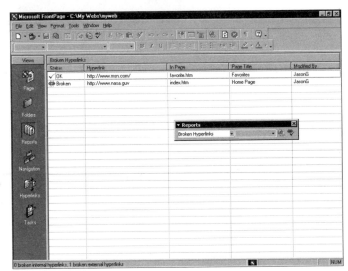

TIP

Replace links in selected pages only. *In the Edit Hyperlink dialog box, click the Change In Selected Pages option button if you don't want to globally replace all occurrences of the link to the web page. Then select the page or pages you want to edit by selecting them in the list box. (Hold down the Ctrl key if you want to select multiple pages.)*

TIP

Use any view. *The Recalculate Hyperlinks command works in all views. It tells the web server to update your hyperlinks and remove references to deleted pages.*

Edit Broken Links

1. Right-click a broken link in the Broken Hyperlinks report.

2. Choose Edit Hyperlink from the shortcut menu.

3. Enter the web page URL in the Replace Hyperlink With text box to specify the correct link. Or click Browse to find the web page.

4. Click the Change In All Pages option button if you want to replace every occurrence of the link with the web page you entered in the Replace Hyperlink With text box.

5. Click Replace.

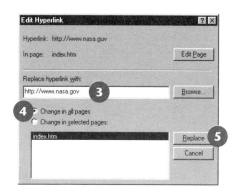

Recalculate Your Web Site's Links

1. Choose Recalculate Hyperlinks from the Tools menu.

2. When FrontPage displays a message box telling you that recalculating repairs hyperlinks, updates components, and synchronizes web data, click Yes.

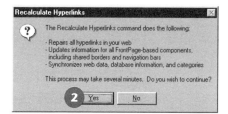

Checking Spelling in a Web Site

Just as you can use FrontPage to check hyperlinks across an entire web site, you can also use FrontPage to check spelling in several or all of your web pages at once by using the same, powerful spell-checker that the Microsoft Office 2000 suite uses.

TIP

Check spelling on one page.
If you're in Page view and you click the Spelling toolbar button, FrontPage will spell-check only the current page.

Spell-Check Your Web Site's Pages

1. In any view other than Page view, click the Spelling toolbar button.

2. Click the Entire Web option button to check the spelling of all your web pages.

3. Click Start.

4. To correct a page immediately, double-click it and then use the Spelling dialog box to correct the misspelled words.

5. To postpone correcting a page's misspellings, select the page and then click Add Task. FrontPage adds this task to your Tasks list.

6. Click Done or Cancel when you're finished.

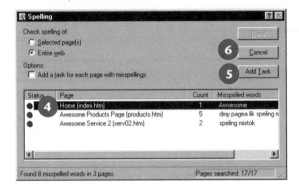

Viewing Web Site Tasks

Even after you've created a framework for your web site, you still have much work to do. To help you keep track of which web pages need to be finalized and where important images need to be replaced, FrontPage includes a To-Do List that you work with in the Tasks view. (When you run one of the web wizards, FrontPage actually builds a preliminary To-Do List for you, consisting of tasks it knows you'll need to accomplish.)

View and Sort the Tasks on Your To-Do List

1. Click the Tasks button on the Views bar.

2. Move the scroll bars up and down or left and right to scroll your list.

3. Click a column heading button to sort the tasks.

Click here to sort by this column.

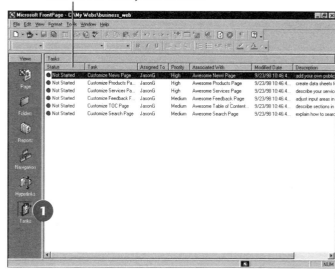

Working with Tasks

FrontPage builds an initial list of tasks that you need to complete, which mostly consists of replacing place-holders with real web content. This initial list, however, is by no means exhaustive, so you will most likely want to add new tasks to it. You might also want to view and edit descriptions of tasks currently on the list.

Add a Task to the Tasks View

1 Click the Tasks button on the Views bar to display the Tasks view.

2 Click the down arrow next to the New toolbar button, and choose New Task from the drop-down menu.

3 Type a name in the Task Name text box.

4 Type a person's name in the Assigned To text box.

5 Select a Priority option.

6 Describe the task in the Description text box.

7 Click OK.

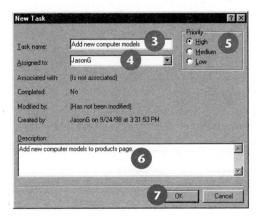

SEE ALSO

See Section 3, "Working with Web Page Text," on page 33 for information on how to edit web pages in FrontPage.

Edit a Task Assignment, Description, or Priority

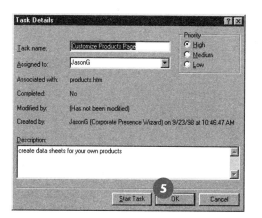

1. Click the Tasks button on the Views bar to display the Tasks view.

2. Right-click the task.

3. Choose Edit Task from the shortcut menu.

4. Edit the task details.

   ◆ Assign the task to a different person by typing a new name in the Assigned To text box.

   ◆ Change the task priority by clicking a different Priority option button.

   ◆ Change the task description by typing new text in the Description text box or by editing the existing text.

5. Click OK.

Completing Tasks

Completing the tasks on your To-Do List is by far the most time-consuming part of building your web site. Completing these tasks involves filling individual web pages with graphic and textual content, which necessarily includes several critical decisions, such as what information to include, how to organize it, and how to lay it out. As you complete tasks, you'll want to mark them off your To-Do List so that you can monitor your progress.

TIP

Completed tasks disappear.
After you mark a task as completed, it disappears from your To-Do List as soon as you leave Tasks view. If you want to see your completed tasks, right-click anywhere in the Tasks view (other than on a task) and choose Show Task History from the shortcut menu.

Perform a Task

1 Click the Tasks button on the Views bar to display the Tasks view.

2 Right-click the task.

3 Choose Start Task from the shortcut menu. FrontPage opens the web page you need to complete the task.

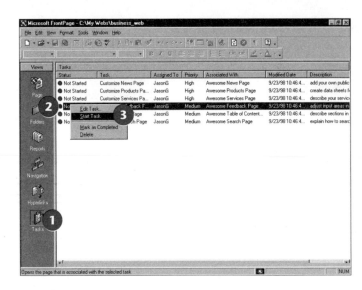

Mark a Task as Completed and Delete a Task

1 Right-click the task.

2 Choose a command from the shortcut menu.

◆ Choose Mark As Completed if you've completed the task

◆ Choose Delete to remove the task. When FrontPage asks you to confirm the delete, click Yes.

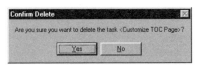

Previewing Your Web Site

Before you publish your web site to your web server, it's usually a good idea to preview your web site in a web browser, just to make sure the pages look the way you want and that the links work properly. By doing this, you can often save yourself a lot of time and sometimes embarrassment.

TIP

Try different window sizes.
Resize your browser window to see how your web site looks in differently sized windows. Some pages that look great in a maximized browser at 800x600 screen resolution won't look so hot in a smaller window or maximized with a screen resolution of 640x480.

SEE ALSO

See "Maintaining Resolution Independence" on page 82 for more information on creating web pages that look good at a variety of window sizes and screen resolutions.

View Your Web Site in a Browser

1. In Page view, select your index.htm file.

2. Click the Preview In Browser toolbar button.

3. Navigate your web site just as you would any other site.

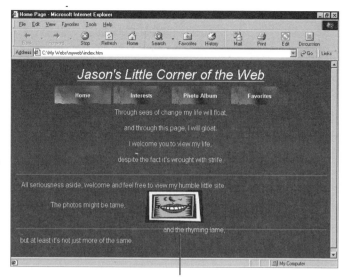

This text doesn't look right when viewed in a maximized browser.

Publishing Your Web Site

Once you've created your web site, edited its pages, checked its hyperlinks, and previewed it in your browser, you're ready to publish it to your web server.

TIP

No capital letters or spaces. *UNIX computers don't deal well with spaces and capital letters, so in the interest of compatibility, FrontPage prohibits publishing to a folder with capital letters or spaces.*

Publish Your Web to a Web Server

1. Choose Publish Web from the File menu.

2. Type the address for your web server, or click Browse to search for it.

3. Select an option to specify whether you want to publish only changed files or all files in your web.

4. Click Publish.

5. Enter your user name and password, and then click OK.

3

Working with Web Page Text

O nce you've created a new web site—remember this is a basic framework of blank web pages ready to fill with content—you can begin creating web page documents. To do this, you fill your web pages with text, images, and other information.

In this section, you'll learn how to fill your pages with textual content—words and numbers. Creating web pages in Microsoft FrontPage is almost the same as creating a document in a word processing program. So if you've used a word processing program before, particularly Microsoft Word, you'll find FrontPage easy to learn and use.

In later sections, you'll learn how to fill your pages with other types of content. Section 4 describes how to work with images, for example. Section 5 describes how you can use special effects, such as sound and video clips, in your web pages.

Where Do I Get the Text?

Good question. Books such as this often skip over the creation of your content, especially the creation of your textual content. They tend to assume that you have all this great information—neatly organized and highly polished, of course—that's just waiting to be dropped into a fancy set of web pages.

For purposes of this section, I have to pretend that you have all this content ready to drop into a set of web pages, too. But, actually, before you start any real work on a web site's pages, you need your content.

Content Development: The Big Picture

I can't really tell you how you create the specific textual information you need. I don't know whether you're trying to web-publish corporate marketing literature, a scary true-crime novel, or information about a worthy nonprofit organization you volunteer for. Nevertheless, I want to remind you that the very first thing you need to do when you begin a web publishing project is to develop your content. If you don't already have your content—and particularly your textual content—you may be putting the cart before the horse.

This information gathering and organizing is actually the hardest part of publishing something on an external or internal web. I mention this here because my experience is that most people ignore the content in their rush to jump onto this particular technology bandwagon. So let me throw in some rules of thumb.

Allow at least a couple of days to create any substantial, information-rich web page that's of, say, magazine-article or magazine-column length. Then you will need another day or two to copy-edit and fact-check one article (just to make sure you don't commit embarrassing grammatical errors or appear uninformed because of a factual mistake). If everything functions like clockwork, that totals about a week of time per web article. For a small web site with a dozen articles, you're probably looking at three months of work.

If you want to publish the equivalent of a 500-page book using an internal or external web, your efforts probably quadruple. In this case, maybe you've got six months of research and writing and another six months of editing. All totaled, then, you're looking at maybe a year of effort.

If you're planning a more substantial web publishing presence or project, the numbers quickly grow even larger. The point I want to emphasize is this: content— the very essence of any good web site—is expensive and time-consuming to produce.

Conventional wisdom says you need to update your web site's content continually if you're going to get people to revisit your web site. Assuming you accept the conventional wisdom—and I think you probably should—that means you need to develop new content on a regular basis to keep bringing people back to the web site for repeat visits. (An exception to this rule about needing to develop new content is when people will use your web site for reference—for example, an online employee manual, product pricing or technical specifications information, and downloadable files [such as for IRS tax forms or Microsoft Windows utilities].)

I don't want to discourage you from publishing web pages on the Internet or an intranet. The technology is here to stay, and it opens up wonderful opportunities for sharing information. I just want you to know that, as crazy as it sounds, web publishing is probably much more like the print publishing or television industries than most people realize. It's the content that really matters—not the method used to deliver the information.

A Content Development Loophole

In fairness, I should alert you to the possibility that you actually do have significant volumes of raw content already developed. Or at least halfway developed. Presumably you or your organization have lots of textual information that's already collected and organized. Product literature. Employee manuals and directories. Perhaps annual reports or newsletters. You know the sort of stuff I'm talking about. You need to look closely at this material to determine its suitability. But it's quite likely that some of this material—the information that customers and employees most often ask for—is suitable for a web site.

Content Development: The Little Picture

If you have little bits of information from here and there that you want to work into your web pages, you can type that content directly in the web page. (I'll talk about this in a minute.) But you want the bulk of your content available in electronic files. That means you want the great majority of your text available as text files or word processing documents. (The word processing documents produced by most word processing programs will work just fine.)

You also want any other content you'll include in your web pages available in electronic, or digital, form. This means that you'll need to either scan any artwork or photographs you want to use or re-create this artwork using a graphics or drawing program. (This section describes how you enter textual content in your web pages. The next section describes how you insert images in your web pages.)

Entering Text in a Page

Once you've created a web site, you're ready to begin filling your pages with text. If you've ever worked with Microsoft Word, you'll find that this process works very much like you would expect. For the most part, you click a location within a web page document to position the cursor, and then you begin typing.

TIP

Background spell-checking. *FrontPage automatically checks your spelling and grammar while you type. Any spelling mistakes are underlined in red; grammatical errors are underlined in green.*

TIP

Convert text to hyperlinks. *If you enter a string of text that FrontPage recognizes as a URL, it will convert the text into a hyperlink to that location.*

SEE ALSO

See "Creating Hyperlinks" on page 38 for more information about hyperlinks.

Open a Web Page

1. Start FrontPage, and open the web site.

2. Double-click the web page you want to open.

Enter New Text

1. Click to place the cursor where you want to add new text.

2. Type the new text in the web page.

3. Press the Enter key to end one paragraph of text and begin another paragraph.

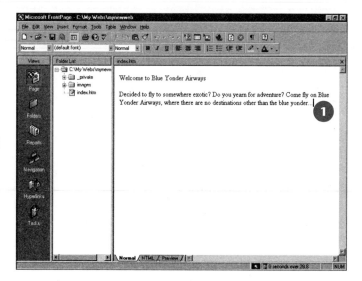

Delete Existing Text

1. Select the text you want to delete by clicking the first character of the text and dragging the mouse to the last character of the text.

2. Press the Delete key.

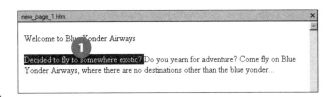

Undo Mistakes

1. If you want to reverse the effect of your last text entry or editing action, click the Undo toolbar button.

2. To undo multiple actions, click the down arrow next to the Undo toolbar button and select the actions from the list.

Replace a Single Occurrence of Existing Text

1. Select the text you want to edit, or change, by clicking the first character of the text and then dragging the mouse to the last character.

2. Type your new text.

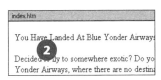

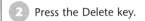

Creating Hyperlinks

Hyperlinks are the most important content of a web page after text. As a web page creator, you will create many hyperlinks. Fortunately, FrontPage makes the task of creating hyperlinks extremely easy.

SEE ALSO

See "Using Bookmarks" on page 96 for more information on hyperlinks to other parts of the same web page.

TIP

Edit existing hyperlinks. *To edit an existing hyperlink, right-click the hyperlink and choose Hyperlink Properties from the shortcut menu.*

Insert a Hyperlink

1 Select the text you want to link to another page or file.

2 Click the Insert Hyperlink toolbar button.

3 If you want to link to a page or file contained in your web site, select the page. Otherwise, enter the URL for the page or file in the URL text box.

4 If the page contains bookmarks, select one from the Bookmark drop-down list box.

5 Click OK.

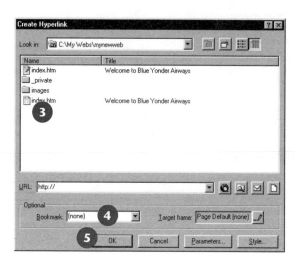

Don't link to your hard drive. *Unless you are publishing your web site to an intranet and everyone on the intranet has access to your own hard drive or network resources, hyperlinks to files or pages on your computer will break as soon as you publish the page. Always link to either files in your web or files on the Internet.*

Link to an FTP site. *To create a hyperlink to a file on an FTP site, type the prefix* ftp:// *before the ftp site to which you want to link. For example, type* ftp://ftp.microsoft.com *for Microsoft's ftp site at* ftp.microsoft.com.

Create Other Types of Hyperlinks

1. Select the text you want to link to another page or file.

2. Click the Insert Hyperlink toolbar button.

3. Click the button corresponding to the type of link you want to create, and type the location of the page or file in the URL text box.

4. Click OK.

Click to use your web browser to select a page.

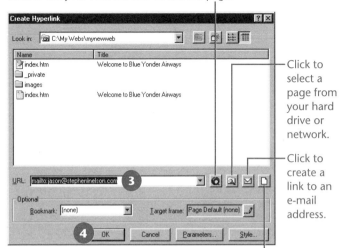

Click to select a page from your hard drive or network.

Click to create a link to an e-mail address.

Click to create a link to a new page.

Internet Protocols and URLs

When you create hyperlinks, FrontPage asks you questions about Internet resource protocols and uniform resource locators (URLs). These questions aren't difficult to answer once you've worked a little with the Internet; however, it's helpful for new users to get a quick overview of exactly what these things are and how they're used.

What Are Internet Protocols?

You can use the word *protocol* in a variety of ways when talking about computers and the Internet. It's important for you, as a web publisher, to think about the word as a way to refer to specific sets of rules for moving information between computers. For example, the World Wide Web uses one set of rules—called the hypertext transfer protocol, or HTTP—for moving information from computer to computer, but the Internet actually uses several other popular protocols for moving information as well, as described in the table shown here.

Because the Internet uses or supports the use of different protocols, FrontPage lets you create hyperlinks that use protocols in addition to HTTP. To create a hyperlink based on a different protocol, all you do is type the protocol prefix in the URL box. The following table lists examples of protocol prefixes you might enter.

INTERNET PROTOCOLS	
Protocol prefix	**What it does**
ftp://	Moves files between computers.
https://	Securely moves web pages between computers so that the information can't be viewed or read by other computers during transmission.
news:	Connects your web browser to a news, or newsgroup, server.
telnet://	Turns your computer into a dumb computer terminal and then connects this dumb terminal to another computer—typically a large mainframe computer.
file://	Works with files stored locally on your computer or local area network.

How URLs Work

Uniform resource locators, or URLs, describe the precise location of an Internet or intranet resource—usually a document or program that you want to use, read, or retrieve. For example, the following is the URL for a page at the Microsoft Corporation web site: *http://www.microsoft.com/misc/features.htm* .

In general, when you create a hyperlink—especially those that describe Internet resources rather than intranet resources—you supply three pieces of information:

- ◆ protocol
- ◆ server name
- ◆ file pathname

The first part of a URL describes the protocol. For example, any World Web Wide URL can and usually should include the *http://* or the *https://* protocol prefix. However, as discussed earlier in this sidebar, you can also create URLs that point to Internet and intranet resources in addition to web sites and web pages. (See the table on page 40 for a partial list of these other resources.)

The second part of a URL names the server where a particular resource resides. This may seem unnecessarily complicated if you're used to working in a personal computer environment, but, in general, remember that sharing information across the Internet or even a small intranet requires two computers or computer networks: a client computer or network (probably your desktop computer) and a server computer or network (the computer or network supplying the resource you want). When you want to get information from the Internet or an intranet,

therefore, you need to give the client computer the name of the server computer from which it's supposed to request the information. If you wanted to grab information from the Microsoft Corporation web site, for example, you would need to supply the web server's name: *www.microsoft.com* .

The third and final part of a URL is the file pathname. This last bit of information specifies both the document or program filename and its location on the server. In the case of the *http://www.microsoft.com/misc/features.htm* URL, for example, features.htm is the file pathname because the HTML document, features.htm, resides in the server's */misc/* directory.

3

Inserting Text Objects

At times, you might want to insert a text object in a web page rather than enter the text by using FrontPage. For example, if you already have a document that you created in a word processing program, you might want to insert it in a web page instead of retyping it. Or you might need to add a symbol or character not on your keyboard (especially if you are creating a multilanguage site).

Insert formatted text. *If FrontPage makes errors in the way it converts a document (this happens most often with spreadsheet documents), try saving the file to a Rich Text Format (.rtf) file first.*

Insert a Text File

1 Click to place the cursor where you want to add new text.

2 Choose File from the Insert menu.

3 Specify the location of the file you want to insert in the Look In drop-down list box.

4 Specify the format of the file you want to insert in the Files Of Type drop-down list box.

5 When FrontPage displays the file in the list box, double-click the file to insert its contents in the web page at the cursor location.

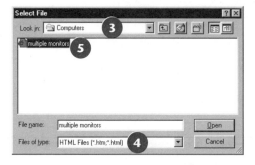

Use a symbol. *Double-click a character in the Symbol box to insert it.*

Insert a Symbol

1 Click in your web page to place the cursor where you want to insert the new symbol.

2 Choose Symbol from the Insert menu.

3 Click the symbol you want to insert. You can insert more than one symbol at a time by clicking additional symbols.

4 Click Insert.

5 Click Close to close the Symbol dialog box.

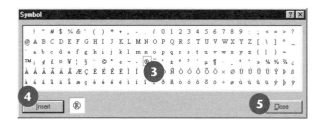

Polishing Your Web Page Prose

FrontPage comes with the Microsoft Office Spelling and Thesaurus tools. After you've entered all your text and made your editing changes, use the spelling tool to find and correct any spelling errors. You may also want to use the Thesaurus tool to polish your prose.

TIP

Check a portion of a page. *To check the spelling in only a portion of the web page, simply select the text you want to spell-check before choosing Spelling from the Tools menu.*

SEE ALSO

See "Checking Spelling in a Web Site" on page 26 for information on how to spell-check across the entire web site.

Spell-Check Your Web Page

1 Choose Spelling from the Tools menu. If FrontPage finds a misspelling, it displays the Spelling dialog box.

2 If FrontPage shows the correct spelling in the Suggestions list box, click the word.

3 If nothing appears in the Suggestions list box and you know the correct spelling, type it in the Change To text box.

4 Click Change to correct only this occurrence of the misspelling. Click Change All to correct this occurrence and every other occurrence of the misspelling.

5 If the word is actually correct to begin with, click Ignore to ignore only this occurrence of the word. Click Ignore All to ignore every occurrence of the word. Or click Add to add the word to the custom dictionary.

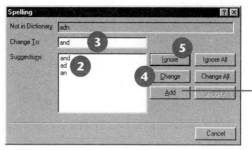

Click Add if you want to add the word to the FrontPage dictionary.

TRY THIS

Find the meaning. *You can look up the meaning of and get synonyms for any word shown in the Thesaurus dialog box by selecting the word in the list and clicking Look Up.*

Use the Thesaurus

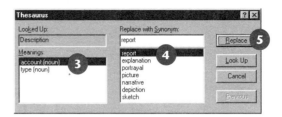

1. Select the word you want to replace with a different word.

2. Choose Thesaurus from the Tools menu.

3. Verify that the Meanings list box shows the correct word definition.

4. Select a word from the Replace With Synonym list box. FrontPage places the selected replacement word in the Replace With Synonym text box.

5. Click Replace.

Moving and Copying Text

FrontPage lets you perform the same cut, copy, and paste operations as does your word processor. This ability to cut, copy, and paste makes it easy to move and copy text within and between web page documents.

Move Text Within a Web Page

1. Select the text you want to move.

2. Click the text selection, and then drag it to the new location.

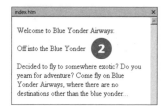

Move Text Between Web Pages

1. Open the files you want to work with by double-clicking them in the Folder List.

2. Select the text you want to move from the first web page window, and click the Cut toolbar button.

3. Choose the page you want to move the text into from the Window menu.

4. Place the cursor where you want to insert the text, and click the Paste toolbar button.

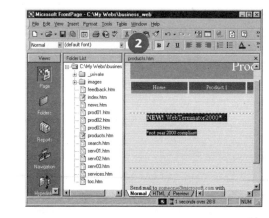

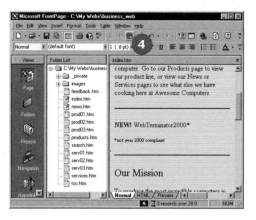

Copy Text Within a Web Page

1. Select the text you want to copy.

2. Click the text selection, hold down the Ctrl key, and then drag the text to the new location.

 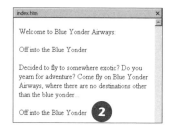

Copy Text Between Web Pages

1. Open the files you want to work with by double-clicking them in the Folder List.

2. Select the text you want to copy from the first web page window, and click the Copy toolbar button.

3. Choose the page you want to copy the text into from the Window menu.

4. Place the cursor where you want to insert the text, and click the Paste toolbar button.

3

Formatting Characters

Once you've entered and polished your web page text, you can then add character-level formatting, such as boldfacing, italics, and underlining. You can also color text and change the font. This character-level formatting makes your web page more legible and more interesting.

Enchanted

TIP

Font compatibility. *If viewers of your web page do not have the font you used installed on their computers, they will be shown their browsers' best approximation of the font you chose, and it's not always that good. Stick with the default font if you want to be safe.*

Add Text Effects

1. Select the text you want to format.

2. Click one of the following toolbar buttons.

   B   Bold

   I   Italic

   U   Underline

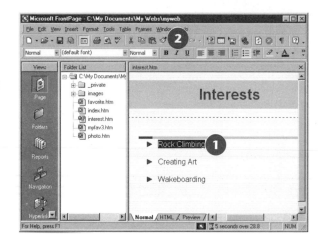

Specify the Font

1. Select the text for which you want to specify a font.

2. Click the Font drop-down list on the Formatting toolbar.

3. Select the font you want to use for the selected text.

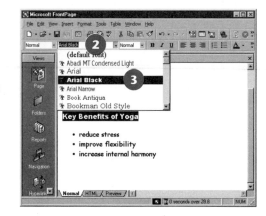

More font options. *You can control all aspects of a font's appearance by choosing Font from the Format menu.*

Remove formatting. *To remove formatting you've added with the Bold, Italic, or Underline toolbar buttons, just select the formatted text and then click the button a second time.*

Web-safe colors. *All colors FrontPage uses will view similarly in other browsers on other types of computers, so the colors are considered web safe. Colors you choose manually from the Custom Colors dialog box may not be web safe, so use them sparingly.*

Color or Highlight Text

1. Select the text you want to recolor or highlight.

2. Click the down arrow next to the Font Color or Highlight Color toolbar button.

3. Click the square that displays the color you want to use for the selected text.

4. Click More Colors if you want to choose a different color.

5. Choose a color, or click Custom to pick a custom color (that may not be web safe).

6. Click OK.

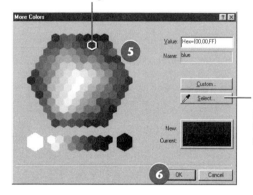

Click a color hexagon to select that color.

Click Select to pick a color from anywhere on your screen.

Creating Headings and Subheadings

To create headings and subheadings within a web page, you use the FrontPage built-in heading styles: Heading 1—the highest-level heading—Heading 2, Heading 3, and so on through Heading 6—the lowest-level heading.

TIP

Be consistent with headings.
It's a good idea to use headings consistently throughout your web site. If you use Heading 1 for your first heading on one page, use it for your first heading on all the pages for a consistent look.

SEE ALSO

See "Working with Style Sheets" on page 58 and "Using Themes" on page 88–89 for information on how to apply a consistent look to your entire web site.

Create a Heading

1. Type the text you want to use as a heading, and then press the Enter key.

2. Select the heading text.

3. Click the Style drop-down list on the Formatting toolbar.

4. Select a heading style.

Click a Paragraph Alignment toolbar button to specify the paragraph alignment.

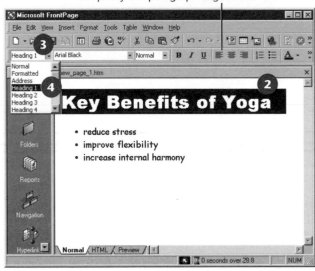

Use higher numbers for subheadings. *Make sure that your headings use a lower-numbered heading style (such as Heading 1 or Heading 2) than your subheadings (which might use Heading 3 or Heading 4).*

Format a style. *To precisely control the heading style, including margins, padding, borders, and many other options, choose Style from the Format menu and then select the text element you want to format: h1 for Heading 1, h2 for Heading 2, and so forth. Click Modify, and in the Modify Style dialog box, click Format, and then choose an aspect of the style from the drop-down menu.*

Create a Subheading

1 Type the text you want to use as a subheading, and then press the Enter key.

2 Select the subheading text.

3 Click the Style drop-down list on the Formatting toolbar.

4 Select a subheading style.

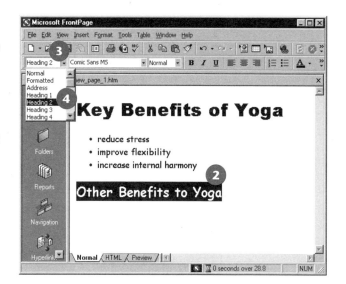

Formatting Paragraphs

FrontPage supports several varieties of paragraph-level formatting—indenting paragraphs, aligning paragraphs horizontally across the page, and even breaking lines within paragraphs. You create paragraphs by entering a block of text and then pressing the Enter key to create a new paragraph.

TIP

Avoid unnecessary line breaks. *Visitors viewing your web page at a different resolution will have different line breaks than the ones you see. Use line breaks to separate text, but don't use them to keep lines of even length. Let the visitors' browsers do that.*

TIP

Display format marks. *To display or hide format marks (the nonprinting page elements, such as paragraph marks), click the Show/Hide All toolbar button.*

Break a Line of Text Without Creating a New Paragraph

1 Click to place the cursor where you want to break a line without creating a new paragraph.

2 Hold down the Shift key while pressing Enter, and FrontPage breaks the line but doesn't create a new paragraph.

Change Paragraph Alignment

1 Select the paragraph you want to align across the page.

2 Click one of the following toolbar buttons.

- Align Left, to align the paragraph against the left edge of the page
- Center, to center the paragraph horizontally
- Align Right, to align the paragraph against the right edge of the page

This nonprinting character is a line break.

Our Mission¶

We want to improve people's lives by maximizing the amount of time they spend in their car. ↵
Since in today's society, a person's car is usually more of a home to them than their actual house or apartment, we want to help empower people to "stay home" by creating more time for them to use their cars. To do this, we are implementing a two-pronged strategy: more traffic, fewer roads.¶

¶

Center button

Align Left button   Align Right button

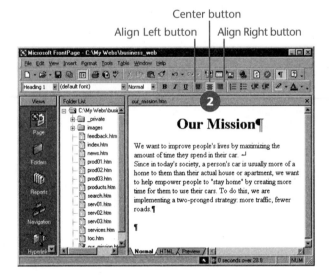

Select a paragraph. *You can select a paragraph by pressing the Alt key and clicking one of the lines of the paragraph.*

Use Format Painter. *You can "paint" one text selection's formatting onto another text selection by selecting the text whose formatting you want to copy, clicking the Format Painter toolbar button, and then selecting the text to which you want to apply the formatting.*

Change Paragraph Indentation

1. Select the paragraph you want to indent or unindent.

2. Click one of the following toolbar buttons.

   ◆ Increase Indent indents the paragraph.

   ◆ Decrease Indent unindents the paragraph.

Decrease Indent button Increase Indent button

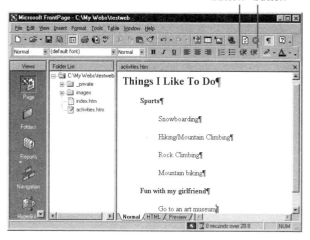

3

Adding Horizontal Lines

Web pages often employ horizontal lines to visually separate the pages into sections. Horizontal lines are not only aesthetically pleasing but they also make long documents easier to read.

TIP

Cut and paste lines. *You can copy, cut, and paste horizontal lines in the same manner as you copy, cut, and paste text selections.*

Insert a Horizontal Line Between Two Paragraphs

1 Place the cursor at the beginning of the paragraph in front of which you want to insert a line.

2 Choose Horizontal Line from the Insert menu.

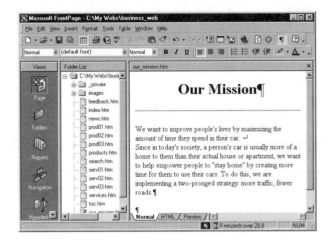

Customize a Horizontal Line

1 Right-click the horizontal line you want to customize.

2 Choose Horizontal Line Properties from the short-cut menu.

3 Specify the width of the line (how long it should be) by using the Width box and option buttons.

4 Specify the height of the line (how thick it should be) in the Height box.

5 Specify the position of the line (whether it's left-aligned, centered, or right-aligned) by clicking an Alignment option button.

6 Select a color for the line from the Color drop-down list box.

7 Select the Solid Line (No Shading) check box if you don't want FrontPage to draw a shadow for the line.

8 Click OK.

Working with Paragraph Lists

You can rearrange a set of paragraphs—remember, a paragraph is just a block of text that ends where you've pressed the Enter key—so that they appear as a numbered list, a bulleted list, or some other specially formatted list.

How to Change Your Oil¶

1. take oil out¶
2. get oil on hands, car, dog¶
3. put oil back in¶

TIP

Change a list to normal text.
To remove the numbering from a set of paragraphs you've turned into a numbered list, select the numbered list and then click the Numbering toolbar button again.

Create a Numbered List

1. Select the paragraphs you want to convert to a numbered list.

2. Click the Numbering toolbar button.

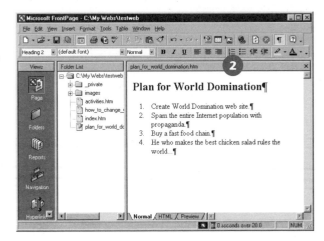

Customize a Numbered List

1. Select the numbered list or the set of paragraphs you want to convert to a numbered list.

2. Choose Bullets And Numbering from the Format menu.

3. Click the Numbers tab.

4. Click the picture you want your numbered list to look like.

5. Optionally, indicate which number FrontPage should use for the first item in the numbered list.

6. Click OK.

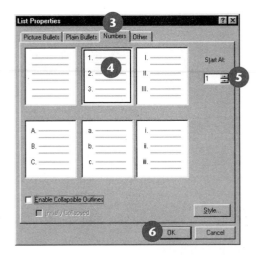

Format text normally. *You can format the text in a numbered list in the same manner as you format other web page text.*

Use images as bullets. *You can tell FrontPage to use some other image for the bullets in your list by clicking the Specify Picture option button on the Picture Bullets tab of the List Properties dialog box and then clicking Browse. FrontPage displays the Select Image dialog box, which you can use to identify an image file and its location.*

Theme bullets. *If your web site uses a theme, the Bullets And Numbering dialog box does not have a Plain Bullets tab.*

Create a Bulleted List

1. Select the paragraphs you want to convert to a bulleted list.

2. Click the Bullets toolbar button.

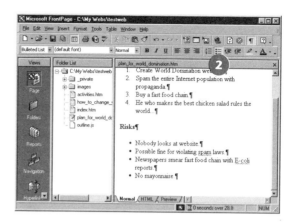

Customize a Bulleted List

1. Select the bulleted list or the set of paragraphs you want to convert to a bulleted list.

2. Choose Bullets And Numbering from the Format menu.

3. Click the Plain Bullets tab.

4. Click the picture you want your bulleted list to look like.

5. Click OK.

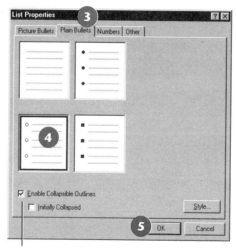

Use these check boxes to enable visitors to collapse your outline

3

Working with Style Sheets

Cascading Style Sheets (CSS), also known simply as style sheets, are a very powerful tool that you can use with FrontPage to create a unified look for your web site. A CSS file is a text file that contains specifications for formatting: what color Heading 1 should be, what font hyperlinks should use, and so forth. You can link your web pages to this CSS file so that all the pages follow the formatting specified in the file.

Create a New Style Sheet

1. In Page View, choose New from the File menu and Page from the submenu.

2. Click the Style Sheets tab.

3. Choose a style sheet from the list, and then click OK.

4. Click the Save toolbar button to save your style sheet.

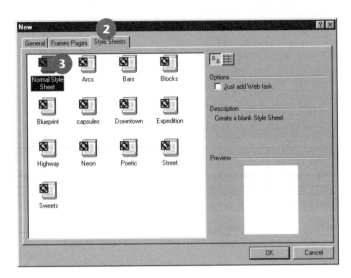

Link Web Pages to a Style Sheet

1. In Folders view, select the pages to which you want your style sheet to apply.

2. Choose Style Sheet Links from the Format menu.

3. Click Add to select the style sheet to link to.

4. Click OK when you're finished.

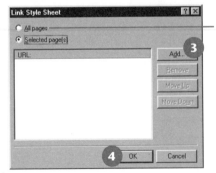

Click this option button to link the style sheet to all pages.

TIP

Style sheet code. *CSS files can look a little scary if you're not used to dealing with code, but they can be read. The style sheet contains style names and their specifications, or properties. Although most people don't read an RGB color value of 255,255,0 and think "blue," if you're patient, you can get the general idea of what the style sheet says.*

TIP

Style sheet compatibility. *Cascading Style Sheets work with only Internet Explorer 3.0 or later and Netscape Navigator 4.0 or later.*

SEE ALSO

See "Using Themes" on page 88–89 for information on the FrontPage preformatted style sheets called Themes.

Edit a Style Sheet

1 Open the style sheet by double-clicking it in the Folder List.

2 Choose Style from the Format menu.

3 Select a style, such as Body for the body text, and click Modify to specify how you want the style formatted.

4 Click Format, and choose an option from the drop-down menu.

5 Modify the style, and click OK when you're finished.

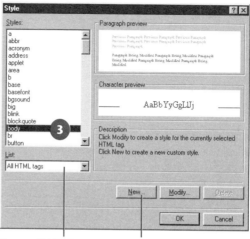

To see all HTML tags, select All HTML Tags here.

Click New to create a new style.

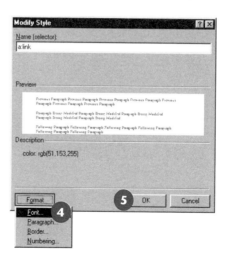

3

Annotating Web Pages with Comments

If you need to write notes to yourself and you don't want your visitors to be able to read them, you can add comments to your web pages.

TIP

Comments are hidden from visitors. *Comments aren't visible when viewed in a web browser. They appear only when you view the document using FrontPage or look at the HTML code itself.*

TIP

Revise comments. *To edit a comment, double-click the comment and add your changes in the Comment dialog box. To delete a comment, select the comment text and press the Delete key.*

Insert a Comment

1. Click in your web page to place the cursor where you want to insert a comment.

2. Choose Comment from the Insert menu.

3. Type the comment you want to add to the web page.

4. Click OK to place the comment at the cursor location.

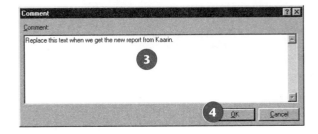

4

Working with Web Page Images

After you've created your web pages and filled them with text—activities described in earlier sections of this book—you're ready to liven up your pages with images. Microsoft FrontPage makes this portion of your web publishing work easy. You'll find that placing images in a web page is much the same as placing images in Microsoft Word documents or Microsoft Excel workbooks. Before you begin placing images in your web pages, however, take a moment to consider what you want to accomplish with your images and how you want to go about your work.

Inserting Images

If you've ever worked with Microsoft Word and have inserted an image, you'll find the process works much the same way in FrontPage. In most instances, you click a location within your web page document to position the cursor, and then you insert the image by clicking the Insert Picture toolbar button.

TIP

Files not in your web. *Click the File button if you want to insert an image file from another location on your computer. Click the World Wide Web button to locate an image on the World Wide Web.*

TIP

File formats. *FrontPage recognizes the following image file types: BMP, EPS, GIF, JPG, PCD, PCX, PNG, RAS, TGA, TIF, and WMF.*

Insert an Image

1. Click to place the cursor where you want to add your image.

2. Click the Insert Picture toolbar button.

3. Double-click the folder containing the image you want to insert, or specify an image on the World Wide Web by typing the image's URL in the URL text box.

4. Select the image from the list box.

5. Click OK to insert the image.

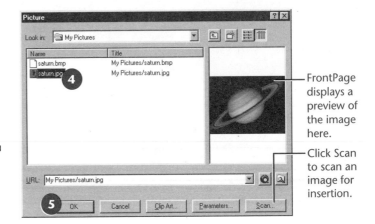

FrontPage displays a preview of the image here.

Click Scan to scan an image for insertion.

TIP

Use the Clipboard. *You can also insert an image from another application by opening the image in the other application, copying it to the Clipboard, and then pasting it into a web page using the Paste toolbar button in FrontPage.*

TIP

Add images to the Clip Art Gallery. *Click the Import Clips button in the Clip Art Gallery to select and add images to the Clip Art Gallery. Or click the Clips Online button to download additional clip art from the Microsoft Office web site.*

Insert an Image from Clip Art

1. Click to place the cursor where you want to add your image.

2. Click the Insert Picture toolbar button.

3. Click Clip Art.

4. Click a category.

5. Click the image you want to insert.

6. Click the Insert Clip button on the pop-up menu.

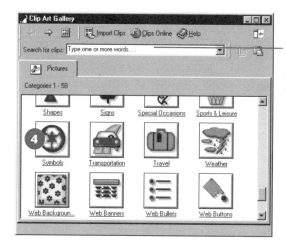

Type a word or phrase to search for a clip.

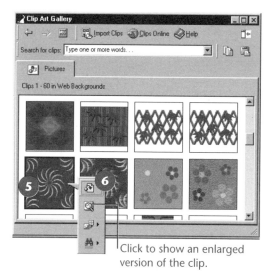

Click to show an enlarged version of the clip.

Using Images Wisely

You can use images, whether photographs or simple illustrations, to add zest to your web site, illustrate a point, or simply make it more fun for people to visit your site. The challenge is to use images wisely while taking into account the opportunities and the limitations they introduce.

Let's start with the most frustrating issue first: the problem of lengthy transmission times. Unfortunately, images take time—sometimes a long time—to load. It's not uncommon for the graphic content of a web page to equal 90 percent of its total size. A 50-kilobyte web page, for example, might contain 5 kilobytes of text and 45 kilobytes of imagery. What that means, of course, is that the graphic content is responsible for 90 percent of the transmission time when a viewer loads a web page. Perhaps that's satisfactory when the imagery represents an important part of the web page content. But those percentages are difficult to defend when the imagery is merely gratuitous. (Note that a 50-kilobyte page takes about 14 seconds to download using a standard 28.8-Kbps modem.) As you add images to your web pages, therefore, you'll want to do so judiciously. Always keep an eye on the download time estimate in the lower right corner of the FrontPage window so that you don't overburden your visitors with unnecessarily slow web pages.

Transmission times represent only one of the challenges of using images wisely, however. Another major challenge you'll encounter is simply making good graphic designs. Although people are quick to add images to web pages (just because they can), producing attractive, graphical web pages is more difficult than most design novices realize. For example, you need to balance the imagery you use for a page so that it doesn't look lopsided or weirdly asymmetrical. You need to work with sets of images that are compatible both within a page and across a web site. In addition, of course, you need to create color schemes that are eye pleasing.

Recognize, too, that people visiting your site may use different size monitors, a variety of display resolutions, and even textual rather than graphical web browsers. So, make sure you consider the full range of visitors who will browse your web site. Check out your site on as many different types of computers as possible. This will give you a feel for how other people are actually seeing your site.

Images created for print publications typically require editing to look good in digital form. Printers use much higher resolutions than do computer screens. Therefore, even though the text content of your printed brochures or annual reports converts easily to a web page, and even though FrontPage expertly converts images to the graphic file formats used in web publishing (GIF and JPEG), you may still need to clean up and resize images if they are to work well on screen and for your web site.

Furthermore, multimedia components such as images occupy a lot of space on the web server, so if you have server space limitations, you'll need to keep this in mind as you add images to your web pages. It's a good idea to delete any images you're no longer using from the web site by right-clicking on them in FrontPage and choosing the shortcut menu's Delete command.

Cropping and Resizing Images

If you need to crop or resize your images, it's always best to do so in an image editing program so that they do not lose quality or become distorted. Nonetheless, you might have to edit your images slightly in FrontPage so that they fit around the text just right.

TIP

Use Auto Thumbnail. *To create a thumbnail sketch (a small version of an image linked to the full version to speed up the download time of a web page), click the Auto Thumbnail button on the Picture toolbar. To set Auto Thumbnail options, choose Page Options from the Tools menu and click the Auto Thumbnail tab.*

Crop an Image

1. Select the image by clicking it.

2. Click the Crop button on the Image toolbar.

3. Drag the selection handles inward to crop the image to the portion you want.

4. Press the Enter key.

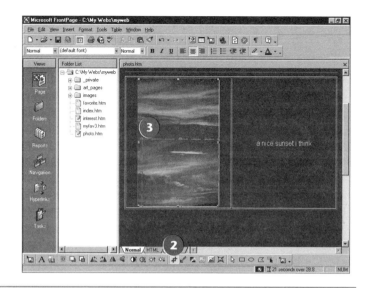

Resize an Image

1. Select the image by clicking it.

2. Drag a corner selection handle outward to increase the image's size. Or drag a corner selection handle inward to decrease an image's size.

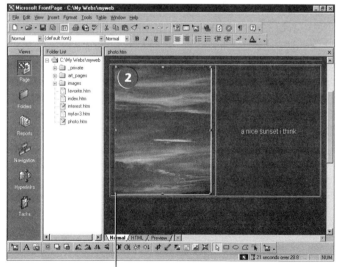

After you select an image, FrontPage adds selection handles to the image.

Copying and Moving Images on a Web Page

After you've placed an image on your web page, you might find that the image doesn't look as you had expected. Luckily, with FrontPage, you can easily move the image around on the page, or you can copy and paste the image so that it doesn't stand alone on the page.

TIP

Undo a mistake. *If you make a mistake and insert the copy of the image in the wrong location, click the Undo toolbar button to undo the paste.*

Copy an Image

1. Select the image by clicking it.

2. Click the Copy toolbar button.

3. Click to place the cursor where you want to add the copy of the image.

4. Click the Paste toolbar button.

Move an Image

1. Select the image by clicking it.

2. Click the Cut toolbar button.

3. Click to place the cursor where you want to move the image.

4. Click the Paste toolbar button.

Here's how the web page fragment looks after moving the image.

Move or Copy an Image with the Mouse

1 Select the image by clicking it.

2 Drag the selected image to its new location.

 ◆ To copy the image, hold down the Ctrl key while you drag it.

 ◆ To move the image, just drag the image to where you want it.

new_page_1.htm

Fun Fall Fashions

This fall I expect to see a burgeoning of color, not just in the trees, but on the streets too. In the following sections, I'll show you what's in store: what's hot, and what's not.

Color Everywhere

new_page_1.htm

Fun Fall Fashions

This fall I expect to see a burgeoning of color, not just in the trees, but on the streets too. In the following sections, I'll show you what's in store: what's hot, and what's not.

Color Everywhere

4

Positioning Images and Placing Text

Once you've inserted your image and resized or cropped it as necessary, you need to position the image properly. You can use FrontPage to wrap text around images, position images anywhere on-screen, and add text to images.

SEE ALSO

See "Maintaining Resolution Independence" on page 82 for information on making sure your web pages look good at different resolutions.

Place Text on an Image

1. Click the image to which you want to add text.

2. Click the Text button on the Picture toolbar.

3. Type your text in the text box.

Click and drag to resize the text box.

Specify How Text Should Wrap

1. Select the image you want to work with by clicking it.

2. Choose Position from the Format menu.

3. Select the option corresponding to the way you want text to wrap around your image, and then click OK.

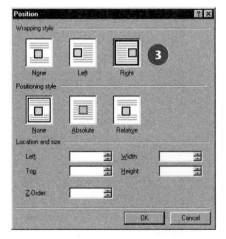

Absolute positioning and resolution independence. *When you position an image using absolute positioning, the image remains in the same location relative to the upper left corner of the screen, regardless of the size of the browser window, which can easily result in a layout different than you intended.*

Use tables for positioning. *You can achieve many of the same effects that absolute positioning allows by putting your text and images in different cells of a table with a border size of 0 to make it invisible.*

Text position. *To change the position of text relative to an image, right-click an image and choose Picture Properties from the shortcut menu. Click the Appearance tab, and select a text alignment option from the Alignment drop-down list box. Note, though, that specifying this text position will clear any other positioning settings, such as wrapped text and absolute positioning.*

Position an Image

1 Select the image by clicking it.

2 Click the Position Absolutely button on the Picture toolbar.

3 Drag the image to any location on screen.

4 Click the Send Backward toolbar button to allow text to flow on top of your image, or click the Bring Forward toolbar button to make your image float on top of text and other graphics.

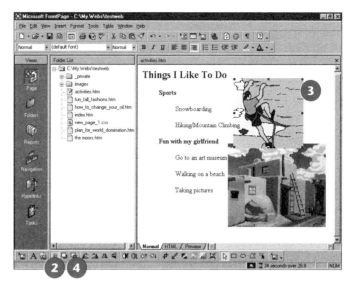

Adding Hyperlinks to Images

Images can do more than just spruce up a page. They can also have hyperlinks attached to them. When visitors click the image, they open the web page or site associated with that image.

TIP

Edit a hyperlink. *You can edit an image hyperlink after you have created it by selecting the image, clicking the Insert Hyperlink toolbar button, and then using the Edit Hyperlink dialog box to specify a new location.*

Create a Hyperlink to a Page in the Current Web

1. Select the image by clicking it.

2. Click the Insert Hyperlink toolbar button.

3. Locate the web page in the list box.

4. Click OK.

TIP

Link to an e-mail address. *To create a hyperlink that sends e-mail, click the E-Mail button and enter the e-mail address in the Create E-Mail Hyperlink dialog box.*

TIP

Link to a new page. *To create a hyperlink to a new page that you want to make, click the New Page button.*

TIP

Check your URL. *Make sure your hyperlink reference is complete. If it is incomplete, FrontPage notifies you that your URL address is bad.*

TIP

Use the status bar. *You can see the embedded hyperlink in the status bar if you move your pointer over the image and then look at the lower left corner of your screen.*

Create a Link to an Internet Resource

1 Select the image by clicking it.

2 Click the Insert Hyperlink toolbar button.

3 Type the URL of the Internet source in the URL box, or click the World Wide Web button to use your browser to locate the Internet source.

4 Click OK.

Test the Image Link

1 Click the Preview tab in FrontPage.

2 Click the image with the hyperlink. FrontPage should display the page to which you linked the image.

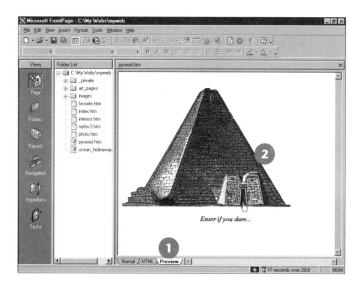

Working with Image Hotspots

Although most image hyperlinks point to a single URL address, it's possible to use an image to point to multiple URL addresses by creating hotspots. You might, for example, have an image showing a map of a state and use each region or county as a hotspot. By clicking within a particular county's borders, for instance, you could display a web page about that county.

Create a Hotspot Hyperlink

1 Select the image by clicking it.

2 Click the Rectangular, Circular, or Polygonal Hotspot button on the Image toolbar.

3 Click and drag within the image to create a hotspot.

4 Locate the page to which you want the hotspot to link.

5 Click OK.

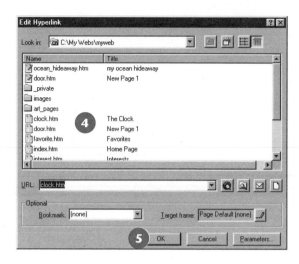

Move a Hotspot

1 Select the image by clicking it.

2 Select the hotspot by clicking the outline.

3 Drag the hotspot to the new location.

Display the Picture toolbar. *To display the Picture toolbar, choose Toolbars from the View menu and Picture from the submenu.*

Select the image. *To see hotspots in FrontPage, you must first select the image.*

Resize a Hotspot

1. Select the image by clicking it.

2. Select the hotspot by clicking the outline.

3. Drag a selection handle to enlarge or shrink the hotspot.

Delete a Hotspot

1. Select the image by clicking it.

2. Select the hotspot by clicking the outline.

3. Press the Delete key.

4

Editing Hotspot Hyperlinks

It is important to periodically check all the links you add to your web pages for the obvious reason that you don't want to mislead your web visitors. If you find that a hotspot hyperlink points to the wrong page, you can edit the hyperlink so that it leads to the correct location. Then once you have made your changes, you can test the new hyperlink before publishing the web site.

SEE ALSO

See "Internet Protocols and URLs" on pages 40–41 for more information on URLs.

Edit a Hotspot's Link

1. Double-click the hotspot you want to relink.

2. Use the list box to select a different page to which you want the hotspot to link, or use the URL box and the buttons beside the box to create a link to a new page or a page outside the current web site.

3. Click OK.

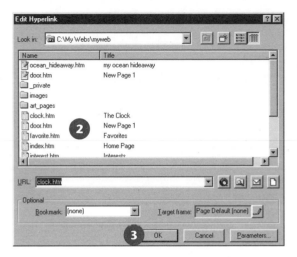

TIP

Use the status bar. *You can see the embedded hyperlink in the status bar. Move your pointer over the image and then look at the lower left corner of your screen. The hyperlink will display.*

Test the Link to a Hotspot

1 Click the Preview tab in FrontPage.

2 Click the hotspot. FrontPage should display the page to which the hotspot points.

Setting Image Alternates

As you create your web site, you need to keep in mind the numerous different ways in which your potential web site visitors browse the web. Some people choose to browse only text so that they can dramatically reduce the time it takes to load web pages. Other people have access to only older versions of browsers or to slow connections. Creating a text-only or low-resolution representation of your image allows all visitors to get a glimpse of what the image represents and peruse your web pages with ease.

TRY THIS

Enclose text in brackets.
Consider enclosing the text-representation text in brackets. For example, if the image is a bullet icon, the text-only representation would be [bullet]. This makes text-only web pages easier to read.

Create a Text-Only Representation of an Image

1. Right-click the image you want to edit.

2. Choose Picture Properties from the shortcut menu.

3. Click the General tab.

4. Type a label that describes the image in the Text box.

5. Click OK.

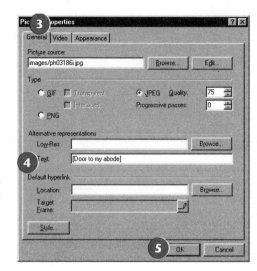

Why text representation is important. *Many people browse web pages without loading the page's images as a way to boost the speed at which the pages load. What's more, many other people only have access to text-only browsers. For these reasons, you'll want to create text representations of your images.*

Keyboard shortcut. *You can also display the Image Properties dialog box by selecting the image and then pressing Alt+Enter.*

Include a Low-Resolution Substitution of an Image

1 Right-click the image you want to edit.

2 Choose Image Properties from the shortcut menu.

3 Click the General tab.

4 Click Browse in the Alternative Representations area.

5 Use the Select Alternate Picture dialog box to locate a low-resolution image you've created.

6 Double-click the image you want to use as an alternate.

7 Click OK.

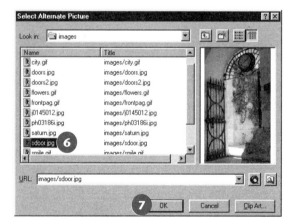

Adding Special Effects to Images

You can change the properties of any element in a web page, including the properties of an image. For example, some images might look better transparent, precisely aligned on the page, or with a border.

Make an Image Transparent

1 Select the image by clicking it.

2 Click the Set Transparent Color button on the Picture toolbar.

3 Click a color of the image that you want to make transparent.

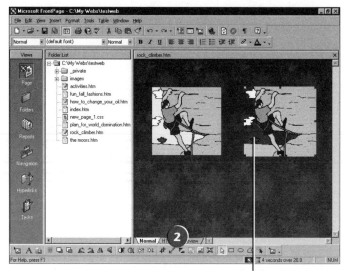

Here's how the image looks after a portion of the image has been made transparent.

Rotate an Image

1 Select the image by clicking it.

2 Click the Rotate or Flip button on the Image toolbar corresponding to the direction in which you want to turn your image.

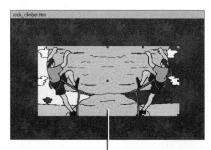

This image has been copied, and then flipped horizontally, creating a mirrored effect.

Add a Border to an Image

1 Right-click the image you want to edit.

2 Choose Picture Properties from the shortcut menu.

3 Click the Appearance tab.

4 Enter a value greater than zero in the Border Thickness box.

5 Click OK.

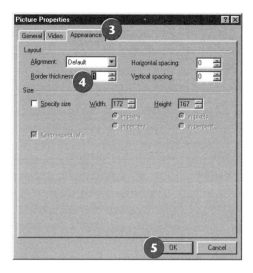

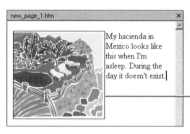

Here's how the image looks after a border has been added.

Changing Image File Format

Depending on the source and content of your image, you might want to change its file format. GIFs in general are better for small graphics, while JPEGs are better for large images and photographs. PNG images are the best for photographs, but they take longer to download and are not as widely compatible as GIFs or JPEGs.

> **TIP**
>
> **Interlaced GIFs and Progressive JPEGs.** *Interlaced GIF graphics and JPEG images with a Progressive Passes setting higher than one appear to visitors to load by layers at a time. Visitors can see a representation of the image before the entire image loads.*

Convert an Image to GIF, JPEG, or PNG Format

1. Right-click the image you want to edit.

2. Choose Picture Properties from the shortcut menu.

3. Click the General tab.

4. Click the option button corresponding to the file type you want.

5. Click OK.

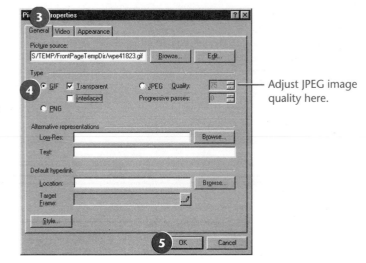

Adjust JPEG image quality here.

5

Managing Web Pages

Earlier in Section 3, "Working with Web Page Text," and Section 4, "Working with Web Page Images," this book described how you create textual and graphic content to fill your web pages with information. This section takes a slightly different approach. It describes how you use Microsoft FrontPage to work with the web pages themselves: how to position objects on a page, how to change the look of a web page, how to add sound and animation, how to print web pages, and how to create templates out of your web pages.

Maintaining Resolution Independence

When you develop a web site, it's important to keep in mind how your audience will be viewing your site. You want your pages to work well with your visitors' browsers, no matter how they are set up. Some people in your audience will be using a standard desktop system much like yours might be, viewing a maximized window at 800x600 resolution and downloading from the Internet with a 56K modem. However, a lot of people use older computers that download at 14.4Kbps, and they view web pages at 640x480 resolution. Some people use their TVs to view web pages and others may use palmtop computers that display at less than 640x480 resolution. A segment of your audience may be blind, in which case they use text-to-speech synthesizers. To reach all of these people, you need to try to maintain resolution independence, as well as provide text versions for everything possible. (See "Setting Image Alternates" on page 76 for information on using text-only representaions of image content. Also see "Using Add Ins" on page 205 for information on making sure your web site is accessible to people with disabilities.)

True resolution independence, or the creation of web pages that look good in any size window, is an almost impossible goal. However, it is possible to do a good job of covering the most often used resolutions without making too many sacrifices. People will always be able to see all of your web pages, even if they view them at a resolution different than what you intended. However, your pages may not have the kind of layout you want.

The most commonly used resolutions today are 640x480 and 800x600, with 1024x768 becoming more widespread as larger monitors become more affordable. These resolutions refer to the number of pixels, or dots, displayed on the screen: at 640x480 there are 640 pixels displayed horizontally and 480 pixels displayed vertically, which together make up the image you see on your screen. If you have an idea what kind of equipment your target audience is using, you can limit the resolutions you need to preview your web site. If you think your target audience is using new computers, create your pages for 800x600 resolution. If you think your audience might be using more modest computers, or even viewing your site with their TVs or handheld devices, you should create your pages for 640x480 resolution.

To develop pages for a specific resolution, it's important to preview your pages often in a browser window that is sized to that resolution. Make sure that navigation bars fit in the window and that your layout isn't dramatically altered by changing the resolution. If you have any sort of advanced formatting, such as images with text wrapped around them, tables, or forms, be sure to test often at different resolutions.

This is what the page looks like at 800x600 resolution.

This text has manual line endings in it.

These images are positioned absolutely and now overlap other items.

This is what the page looks like at 640x480 resolution.

Using Position Boxes

You can use Position Boxes in FrontPage to group text and images anywhere you want on screen. Position Boxes can be very useful when it's important to have a precise layout or to ensure that text and objects don't shift position at different resolutions.

TIP

Arrange Position Box content absolutely. *Use absolute positioning inside a relatively positioned Position Box to maintain a fixed layout inside the box. Use relative positioning for the layout of the separate elements on a page to accommodate different screen resolutions*

Create a Position Box

1. Select the text and/or images you want to include in the Position Box.

2. Choose Position from the Format menu.

3. Click the absolute or relative image to specify how you want your Position Box to be positioned, and then click OK.

4. Click the selection handles to resize the box.

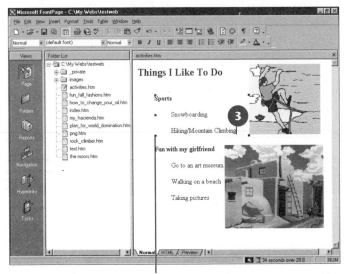

Click here to resize the Position Box.

Layer Position Boxes

1. Drag an absolutely positioned Position Box or image on top of another object.

2. Choose Position from the Format menu.

3. Enter a number in the Z-Order text box. A higher number places the image on top of other images.

4. Click OK.

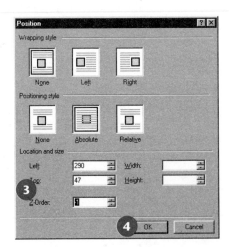

Adding the Date and Time

It's often useful to insert the date and time on a web page to inform visitors when the page was last updated. You can use the FrontPage Date And Time feature to have FrontPage automatically update the information on your web page every time you edit the page.

Insert the Date and Time

1. Type the text you want to precede the date and time.

2. Choose Date And Time from the Insert menu.

3. Select date and time formats from the drop-down list boxes.

4. Click OK.

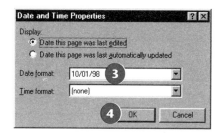

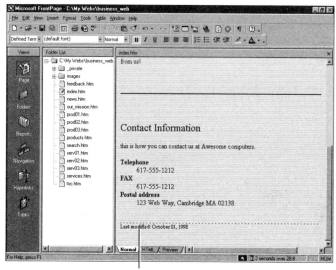

This is how the date looks in a web page.

5

Changing Web Page Colors

Although the default colors for a web page often work well, sometimes you need to change the colors to improve readability or to match the colors in your images.

SEE ALSO

See "Working with Style Sheets" on page 58 for information on changing the style of different elements of a web page.

TIP

Backgrounds that don't scroll. *Select the Watermark check box to make your background image immovable. The text will scroll as if it floats on the background.*

TIP

Set options from another page. *To make your web page background look like that of another web page, select the Get Background Information From Another Page check box, click Browse, and then select the web page you want to copy from. Click OK when you're finished.*

Change Colors

1. Open the web page in which you want to add background color.

2. Choose Background from the Format menu.

3. Select the colors you want from the drop-down list boxes.

4. Click OK.

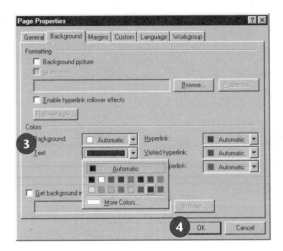

Specify a Background Image

1. Open the web page in which you want to add a background image.

2. Choose Background from the Format menu.

3. Select the Background Picture check box.

4. Type the image name and location in the text box, or click Browse to locate the file.

5. Click OK.

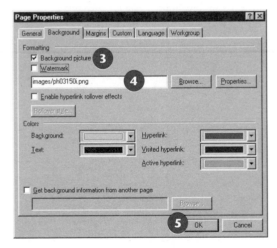

Applying Borders and Shading

You can emphasize any paragraph or object by creating a border around it using the FrontPage Borders And Shading tool.

SEE ALSO

See "Creating Tables" on page 101 for information on using tables to organize information in your web page.

Create a Border

1. Select a paragraph or image.

2. Choose Borders And Shading from the Format menu.

3. Click a Box setting, and select the style of border you want.

4. Specify the width of the borders.

5. To turn off parts of the border, click buttons in the Preview area.

6. Click the Shading tab, and select the colors you want to use.

7. Optionally, specify a background image by clicking Browse.

8. Click OK.

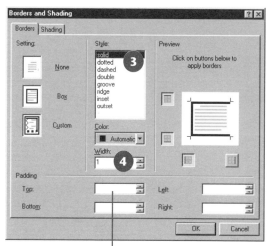

Set the margins for your border.

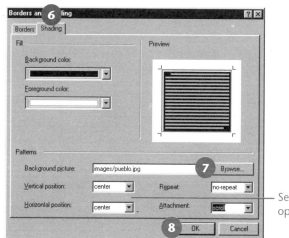

Set image options.

Using Themes

FrontPage includes 60 collections of bundled color and graphics schemes called themes that you can use for individual web pages or for your entire web site. Using themes is a quick way to make your web pages more visually appealing to your visitors.

TIP

Change an existing theme. *You can change the theme on a page the same way you apply a theme to a new page.*

Apply a Theme

1. Open the web page in which you want to use a theme.

2. Choose Theme from the Format menu.

3. Click an option button to apply the theme to all the pages or only selected pages in your web site.

4. Select a theme from the list box to preview it in the box on the right.

5. Select check boxes to alter the selected theme slightly.

   ◆ Vivid Colors makes the colors used more vivid.
   ◆ Active Graphics makes the graphics more eye catching.
   ◆ Background Picture includes a background picture.
   ◆ Apply Theme Using CSS creates the theme using Cascading Style Sheets.

6. Click OK.

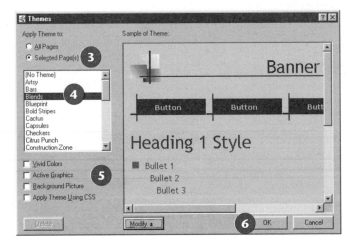

Create a Custom Theme

1 Select a theme, and then click Modify.

2 Click Colors to modify the theme's color scheme.

3 Select a color scheme, or use the Color Wheel and Custom tabs to select your own colors. Click OK.

4 Click Graphics to modify the theme's graphics.

5 Select a graphic item from the Item drop-down list box, and use the Picture and Font tabs to customize the graphic. Click OK.

6 Click Styles, and use the Item and Font list boxes to modify the font for body text and headings. Click OK.

7 Click Save As, and type the name of your scheme. Click OK.

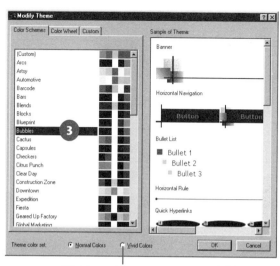

Click to make your pages more vivid.

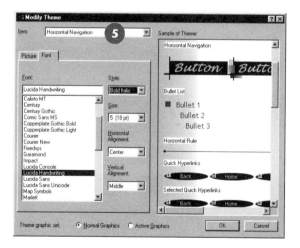

Using Shared Borders

FrontPage lets you create one set of web page borders with information such as a title bar for the page and contact information, as well as navigation buttons, that can be applied to all the pages in your web site or just one particular page. FrontPage calls the borders "shared borders" because you can create one set for all the pages in your web site to share.

TIP

Use shared borders instead of frames. *Many webmasters prefer to use shared borders instead of frames pages because they load faster, work with all web browsers, and are easier to navigate with. However, shared borders remain static on a page, and they can scroll out of view on large pages.*

SEE ALSO

See "Creating Frames Pages" on page 122 for information on creating frames.

Create Shared Borders

1. Open the web site or web page to which you want to add shared borders.

2. Choose Shared Borders from the Format menu.

3. Click an option button to apply the borders to all the pages or just your current page.

4. Select check boxes to indicate where you want borders to appear.

5. Click OK.

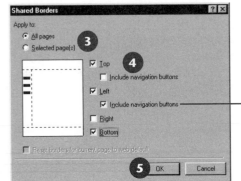

Select this check box to add navigation buttons.

Edit Shared Borders

1. Open a page to which you've added shared borders.

2. Click one of the shared borders boxes, and then edit the border.

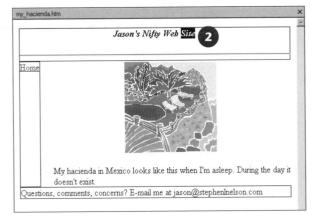

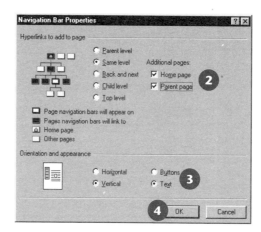

TIP

Add pages to the Navigation view. *In order for automatically generated items such as navigation bars and Page Banners to work, you need to add to the Navigation view any pages on which you want the items to work.*

TIP

Themes and Page Banners. *When you apply a theme to your web page or web site, a graphic will appear behind your Page Banner, creating a title bar effect.*

Edit Navigation Bars

1 Double-click a navigation bar, or choose Navigation Bar from the Insert menu.

2 Select which pages you want to appear.

3 Select how you want your links to appear.

4 Click OK.

Insert Page Banners

1 To add a Page Banner to your top shared border, click the top shared border.

2 Choose Page Banner from the Insert menu.

3 Click an option button to have the Page Banner appear as text or as an image.

4 Type the text you want to appear on the Page Banner.

5 Click OK.

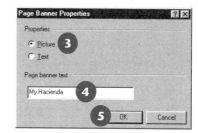

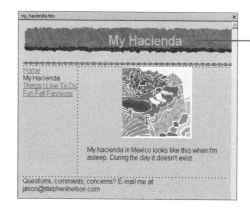

This is the Page Banner.

Adding Sound and Video

Adding sound and video to a web page can make the page much more lively. Just make sure the sound or video clips you add don't take too long to download.

TIP

Don't loop a sound forever. *Looping most sounds forever is a sure-fire way to get your visitors to either leave your web site or turn off their speakers.*

Insert a Background Sound

1. Open the web page in which you want to add background sound.

2. Choose Background from the Format menu.

3. Click the General tab, and then click Browse to locate the sound file.

4. Specify how many times you want your sound to play after the user browses to the page.

5. Click OK.

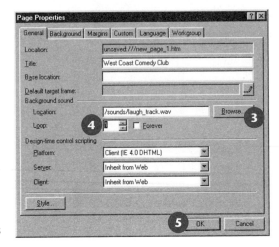

Insert a Video Clip

1. Open the web page in which you want to add a video clip.

2. Choose Picture from the Insert menu and Video from the submenu.

3. Select the video clip file you want to insert.

4. Click OK.

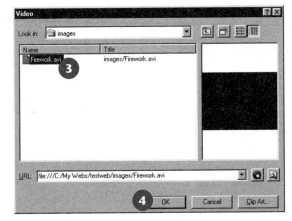

Set an alternate representation. *Make sure to specify an image and text representation of any videos you put on your web page. To do this, right-click the video, choose Picture Properties from the shortcut menu, and then click the General tab.*

Set Video Clip Properties

1. Right-click a video clip, and choose Picture Properties from the shortcut menu.

2. Select the Show Controls In Browser check box to show a small set of video controls on your web page.

3. Specify the number of times you want the video to play in the Loop box.

4. Select a check box to specify when you want the video to start.

5. Click OK.

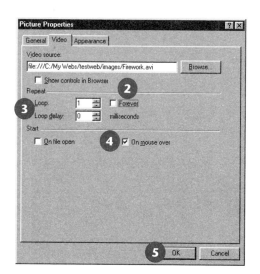

Adding Dynamic HTML Effects

You can use Dynamic HTML (DHTML) to create text and graphics that fly across your web page or respond to a user's mouse actions.

TIP

DHTML works in Navigator and Internet Explorer.
DHTML effects you create in FrontPage appear the same whether you view the page in Netscape Navigator, version 4.0 or higher, or Microsoft Internet Explorer, version 3.0 or higher. If you use an older version of either program, you won't see any animation or interactivity.

Add a DHTML Effect

1. Select the text or image to which you want to add an effect.

2. Choose Dynamic HTML Effects from the Format menu to open the DHTML Effects toolbar.

3. Click the On drop-down list to select when the effect should occur.

4. Click the Apply drop-down list to select the action you would like to apply.

5. Click the Effect Settings drop-down list to select any details associated with the action.

Click to remove any DHTML effects.

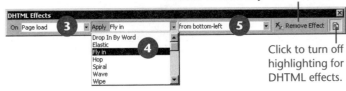

Click to turn off highlighting for DHTML effects.

Adding Page Transitions

Page Transitions let you create movie-style fades and wipes for your visitors to see when they enter or exit your web page. You might want to use Page Transitions if you're creating an online presentation or a series of web pages in which you want to enhance the feeling of interactivity.

Add a Page Transition

1. Open the web page to which you want to add a transition.

2. Choose Page Transition from the Format menu.

3. Select a transition occurrence time from the Event drop-down list box.

4. Select a transition from the Transition Effect list box.

5. Specify the duration of the transition.

6. Click OK.

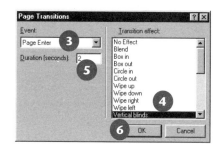

Using Bookmarks

Bookmarks make it easy to move around within a particular web page or to more precisely control where visitors land when they move to the page. Bookmarks, then, work as navigation tools you use within a web page—just as hyperlinks work as navigation tools you use between web pages.

TIP

Select your text. *If you want to place a bookmark at a heading, select the text, and choose Bookmark from the Insert menu. The selected text appears as the bookmark name.*

TIP

Pick a good name. *Use self-descriptive names for your bookmarks—perhaps the names of the web page sections they mark, for example. By doing so, you'll find them much easier to work with later on.*

Create a Bookmark

1. Open the web page in which you want to place the bookmark.

2. Click to place the cursor where you want to insert the bookmark.

3. Choose Bookmark from the Insert menu.

4. Type a name for the bookmark in the Bookmark Name text box.

5. Click OK.

Remove an Existing Bookmark

1. Open the web page with the bookmark.

2. Choose Bookmark from the Edit menu.

3. Select the bookmark from the Other Bookmarks On This Page list box.

4. Click Clear.

Click to go to the selected bookmark.

Printing Web Pages

Unlike word processing documents, which are by definition well-suited for printing on paper, the web pages you create in FrontPage are primarily designed for posting on a web. However, it is often useful to print out a copy of a web page for edit and review.

TIP

Web pages and printed page count. *A web page isn't equal to a single page of paper. A single web page may actually print on several pieces of paper.*

TIP

Printer properties. *To change the paper size, print orientation, or resolution, choose Page Setup from the File menu and then click Options to access your printer's advanced settings and specify how you want your pages to print.*

Print a Web Page Document

1. Open the web page you want to print.

2. Choose Print from the File menu.

3. Select the printer you want to use.

4. Indicate how many pages of the web page document you want to print.

5. Specify how many copies of the web page document you want to print.

6. Click OK to begin printing.

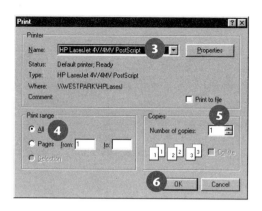

Preview a Printed Web Page Document

1. Open the web page you want to print.

2. Choose Print Preview from the File menu.

3. Click Next Page and Prev Page to move through the document you want to print.

4. Click Close to close the Print Preview window.

5. Click Print to print the document.

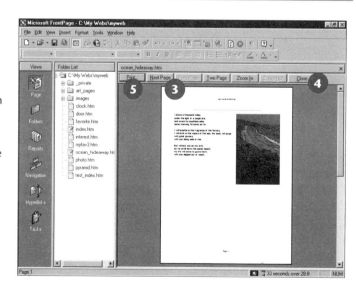

Saving Web Pages as Templates

If you create a web page design that you especially like, you can save the page as a template and then use the template as a base for other pages you create. This feature can be very useful if you frequently create a particular type of page.

TIP

Replace an existing template. *To use the web page as a replacement for a template you already created, click Browse. Then when FrontPage displays a list of the existing templates, double-click the one you want to replace with the new web page template you created.*

TIP

Find a template. *After you save a web page as a template, the template appears in the New dialog box with the list of other web page templates and wizards.*

Save a Web Page as a Template

1. Open the web page from which you want to make a template.

2. Choose Save As from the File menu.

3. Type the filename you want to use for the template.

4. Select FrontPage Template from the list.

5. Click Save.

6. Describe the template in detail—perhaps why you've created the template or for what purposes the template can be used.

7. Click OK.

8. If you don't want to save some of the images on the page along with the HTML document, select the images you don't want to save and click Set Action. Then click the Don't Save option button.

Click to save the template in your current web.

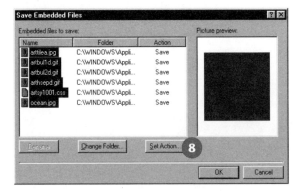

6

Working with Tables

Some of the information you may want to include on your web pages might not fit neatly into paragraphs of text or simple lists. In these situations, you'll need to reorganize your information so that it does fit concisely and legibly on a page. One of the most practical tools available to you is a table, which presents information using a grid of columns and rows. Microsoft FrontPage lets you create tables for your web pages with ease and speed.

A Few Words on Table Basics

Tables aren't difficult to use or understand. In fact, if you're a regular user of Microsoft Word or Microsoft Excel, you already know most of what you need to know. But let's quickly cover the basics.

Tables arrange information into columns and rows of data. Each column-row intersection is called a cell. You use cells to hold the table data. Table cells can hold a variety of data: text, numeric values, images, and even other tables.

The Parts of a Table

Table cells can hold text, numbers, graphics images, and even other tables.

Tables use columns and rows to organize your information.

Cell padding refers to how much space shows between the cell contents and the cell edge.

A table border is the line drawn around the outside edge of the table.

Cell spacing refers to the space drawn between the cells inside the table.

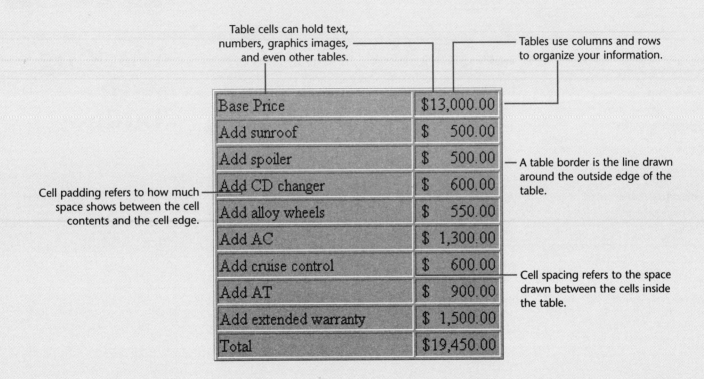

Base Price	$13,000.00
Add sunroof	$ 500.00
Add spoiler	$ 500.00
Add CD changer	$ 600.00
Add alloy wheels	$ 550.00
Add AC	$ 1,300.00
Add cruise control	$ 600.00
Add AT	$ 900.00
Add extended warranty	$ 1,500.00
Total	$19,450.00

Creating Tables

To create a table, you first need to open the web page in which you want to place the table. Once you've done this, you're ready to use the commands on the Table menu and a variety of other techniques to create the table and then fill it with data.

TIP

Table toolbar. *Microsoft FrontPage 2000 has a Table toolbar that often comes in handy when working with tables. To see the toolbar, choose Toolbar from the View menu and Table from the submenu.*

TIP

Resize tables. *To resize any part of a table, place your mouse cursor over the border you want to move. When the cursor changes to a double-sided arrow, click and drag the border to resize the table or part of the table.*

Insert a Table

1. Click the Insert Table toolbar button.

2. Drag the mouse down to specify how many rows you want in your table.

3. Drag the mouse to the right to specify how many columns you want in your table.

4. Click the bottom right square to create the table.

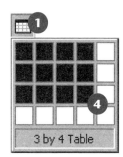

3 by 4 Table

Draw a Table

1. Choose Draw Table from the Table menu.

2. Drag the mouse from the point where you want the top left corner of the table to the point where you want the bottom right corner of the table.

3. Drag the mouse from one side of the table to the other to create rows or from top to bottom to create columns.

4. Click the Draw Table button on the Table toolbar when you're finished drawing the table.

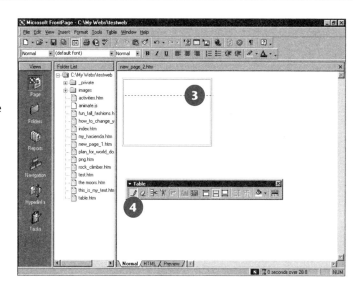

6

Selecting Cells

After you create a table, you may need to select some of the cells, perhaps to clear all their contents or to format them differently from the rest of the table.

Select a Column or Row

1 Click the top border above the column you want to select, or click the side border of the row you want to select.

Select Individual Cells

1 Hold down the ALT key, and click in a cell.

2 Hold down the CTRL key, and click on any other cell to select it. Click it again to deselect it.

Adding Cells to Tables

After you've created a table, you may need to add another cell or two or even entire rows or columns of cells to accommodate more information. You can quickly accomplish all three of these tasks using the insertion commands on the Table menu.

TIP

FrontPage moves other cells right. *When FrontPage inserts a new cell in a table, it moves the other cells in the row to the right.*

TIP

Insert above the selection. *If you want to insert a row above the selected row, click the Above Selection option button.*

Insert a New Cell in a Table

1 Click a cell in the row and column where you want to insert the new cell.

2 Place the cursor where you want to insert the new cell.

3 Choose Insert from the Table menu and Cell from the submenu.

Insert a New Row or Column in a Table

1 Click a cell in the row or column where you want to insert a row or column.

2 Choose Insert from the Table menu and Rows Or Columns from the submenu.

3 Click an option button to insert a row or a column.

4 Specify the number of rows or columns you want to insert in the Number Of Rows or Number Of Columns box.

5 Select a Location option, if necessary.

6 Click OK.

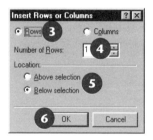

6

Combining and Splitting Cells

Sometimes you might want the contents of a single cell to span across two or more cells. Or you might want to divide a single cell into two or more cells to better fit the data you're showing in a table. To combine and split cells in situations like these, you use the Merge Cells and Split Cells commands on the Table menu.

TIP

Combined cells are placed on separate lines. *When you combine table cells, FrontPage places the contents of each of the original cells onto a separate line of the new cell.*

SEE ALSO

See "Selecting Cells" on page 102 for information on selecting cells in a table.

Combine Two or More Cells

1. Select the cells you want to combine.

2. Choose Merge Cells from the Table menu.

Split a Cell into Two or More Cells

1. Click the cell you want to split into two or more cells.

2. Choose Split Cells from the Table menu.

3. Click an option button to split the cell into columns or rows.

4. Specify how many columns or rows the selected cell should be split into in the Number Of Columns or Number Of Rows box.

5. Click OK.

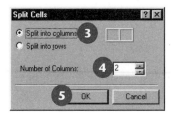

Creating Table Captions

A table caption tells the viewer exactly what you're trying to represent in the table. Table captions also provide a name to use when referencing the table

TRY THIS

Move a caption. *To move a caption to the bottom of the table, right-click the caption and then choose Caption Properties from the shortcut menu. When FrontPage displays the Caption Properties dialog box, click the Bottom Of Table option button.*

Insert a Caption

1 Click the table you want to label with a caption.

2 Choose Insert from the Table menu and Caption from the submenu.

3 Type the caption you want to use to label the table.

Delete a Caption

1 Click to the left of the caption text to select the line the caption is on.

2 Press the Delete key.

6

Deleting Cells from Tables

After you've filled in your table, you might find that you created it with one or two columns or rows too many. This is easy to fix, however, by deleting the row, column, or individual cell from the table. If you are unsatisfied with your table altogether, you can delete the entire table. Likewise, you can delete an entire table from within a table.

Delete a Cell

1. Select the cell you want to delete.

2. Choose Delete Cell from the Table menu.

This is how the table looks before the cell deletion.

This is how the table looks after the cell deletion

Use the Cut button. *Once you've selected your rows, columns, or table, click the Cut toolbar button to remove the selection from your page. If you decide you want the selection later, just click the Paste toolbar button.*

Delete a Row or Column

1️⃣ Select the row or column you want to delete.

2️⃣ Right-click the selection.

3️⃣ Choose Delete Cells from the shortcut menu.

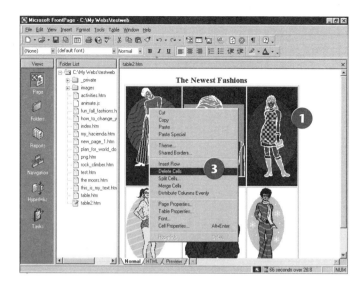

Delete a Table

1️⃣ Choose Select from the Table menu and Table from the submenu.

2️⃣ Press the Delete key.

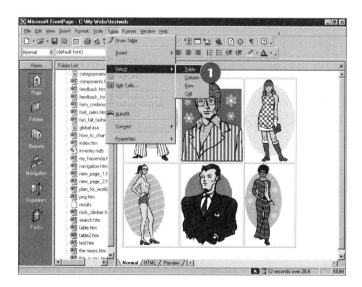

6

Filling a Table with Information

Once you've created a table to hold your information, you're ready to begin filling the individual table cells with text, numbers, and even images. This process works very much like you might expect. You click the cell in which you want to place information. Then you enter that information.

TIP

Edit normally. *You can use all the same editing techniques in a table cell that you use in a web page.*

TRY THIS

Move text by dragging. *You can also drag text and numbers from one table cell to another.*

Enter Text or a Number in a Table Cell

1. Click the table cell.

2. Type the text or number you want in the cell.

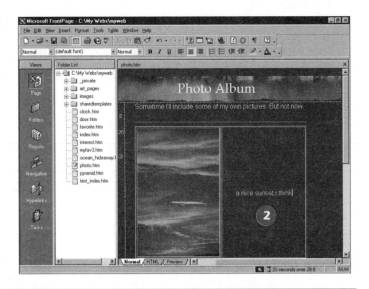

Copy and Move Data Between Table Cells

1. Click the cell with the text or number you want to copy.

2. Select the cell's contents by dragging the mouse from the first character to the last character.

3. Click the Copy toolbar button to copy text. Or click the Cut toolbar button to move text.

4. Click the cell in which you want to paste the text or number.

5. Click the Paste toolbar button.

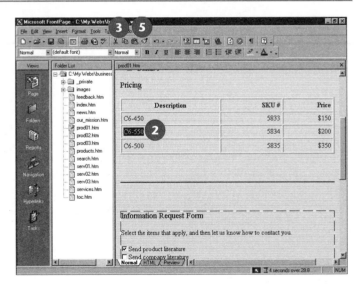

Adding Images to Tables

Tables traditionally hold textual and numerical data, but you can also include images in your tables to spruce them up a bit. You add images to table cells in the same way that you add images to any other location on a web page.

SEE ALSO

See "Inserting Images" on page 62 for more information on adding images to web pages.

TIP

Position images in tables. *Tables make an excellent tool for positioning images and text together. If you don't want to see the border of the table, right-click the table, choose Table Properties from the shortcut menu, and then set the border size to 0.*

Insert an Image in a Table Cell

1 Click the table cell.

2 Click the Insert Picture toolbar button.

3 Select your images folder from the Look In drop-down list box.

4 Select the image you want to insert.

5 Click OK.

Click here to insert a piece of clip art.

Click here to locate an image on your computer.

6

Deleting Cell Contents

If you erroneously enter contents in a cell, you can easily edit the contents or delete them completely.

Delete Text or Numbers in a Table Cell

1. Click the cell with the text or number you want to remove.

2. Select the cell's contents by dragging the mouse from the first character to the last character.

3. Press the Delete key.

Description	2	SKU #	Price
C6-450		5833	$150

Delete an Image in a Table Cell

1. Click the cell with the image you want to remove.

2. Select the image by clicking it.

3. Press the Delete key.

Changing a Table's Background

By adding color and graphic content to your tables, you can capture your visitors' attention and make your tables more exciting to look at.

Files in other locations.
If the background image you want to use is not in the current web site, in the Select Background Picture dialog box click the buttons next to the URL box to locate the image on the World Wide Web or your computer.

Color the Table Background

1. Right-click the table.

2. Choose Table Properties from the shortcut menu.

3. Open the Background Color drop-down list box, and then select a color.

4. Click OK.

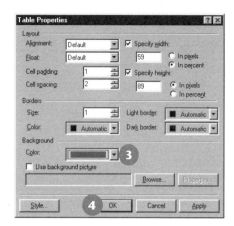

Use an Image for the Table Background

1. Right-click the table.

2. Choose Table Properties from the shortcut menu.

3. Select the Use Background Picture check box.

4. Click Browse.

5. Select the image you want to use by double-clicking an image in the Select Background Picture dialog box.

6. Click OK.

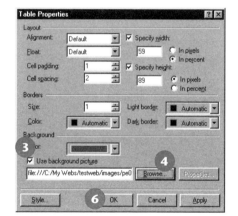

6

Changing a Table's Layout

After you've created a table and filled it with information, you'll probably want to make changes to the table's appearance. Fortunately, this isn't difficult to do because FrontPage gives you control over the appearance of your tables. For instance, if your table lists numerical data, you might want to right-align the cell contents so that the digits line up. You can also change a table's border size or the spacing between the cells to make the table stand out and to make it easier to read.

Change the Alignment of Table Cell Contents

1. Select all rows in a table, and then right-click the table.

2. Choose Cell Properties from the shortcut menu.

3. Select the alignment you want to use from the Horizontal Alignment drop-down list box: Left, Right, or Center.

4. Click OK.

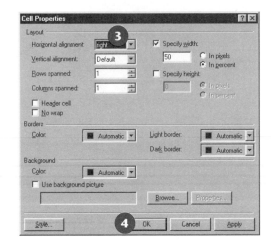

Change the Border Thickness of the Table

1. Right-click the table.

2. Choose Table Properties from the shortcut menu.

3. Specify the table border thickness (in pixels) in the Size box.

4. Click OK.

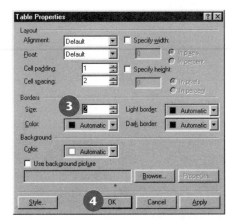

Change the Cell Size in the Table

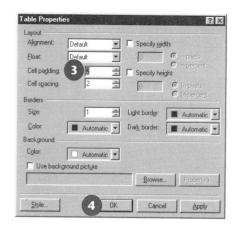

1. Right-click the table.

2. Choose Table Properties from the shortcut menu.

3. Specify the space between the contents of a cell and the sides of the cell (in pixels) in the Cell Padding box.

4. Click OK.

SEE ALSO

See "The Parts of a Table" on page 100 for more information on what cell spacing and cell padding means.

Change the Cell Spacing in the Table

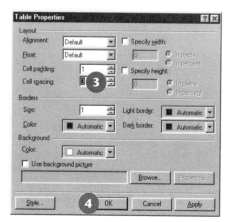

1. Right-click the table.

2. Choose Table Properties from the shortcut menu.

3. Specify the amount of space between the cell borders (in pixels) in the Cell Spacing box.

4. Click OK.

6

Changing a Table's Border Colors

There are two different ways you can color the borders of a table. You can color all the borders with the same color, or you can use two (preferably complementary) colors to give the table a drop-shadow effect.

TIP

Dark border settings. *The Borders Color drop-down list box's setting has no effect on your table borders if you use the Dark Border and Light Border settings.*

TIP

Create shading. *You use the colors specified by the Dark Border and Light Border drop-down list boxes to create the illusion of shading.*

Color All the Table's Borders with One Color

1 Right-click the table.

2 Choose Table Properties from the shortcut menu.

3 Select a color for all the table's borders from the Border Color drop-down list box.

4 Click OK.

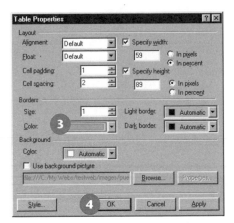

Color the Table's Borders with Different Colors

1 Right-click the table.

2 Choose Table Properties from the shortcut menu.

3 Select a color for the table's top and left exterior and bottom and right interior borders from the Light Border drop-down list box.

4 Select a color for the table's bottom and right exterior and top and left interior borders from the Dark Border drop-down list box.

5 Click OK.

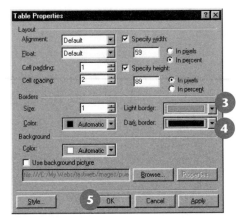

Changing a Table's Width

How well the table fits in the web page and with the rest of the page's content is yet another detail you need to consider. If possible, for example, you want to avoid making your web page visitors scroll back and forth to see the right and left sides or top and bottom of a table in your web page.

TIP

Resolution independence. *As you set your table width, keep in mind that visitors will use different monitor sizes and desktop areas.*

Change the Width of the Table

1 Right-click the table.

2 Choose Table Properties from the shortcut menu.

3 Select the Specify Width check box.

4 To specify the table width in pixels, click the In Pixels option button. Then enter a value in the text box.

5 To specify the table width as a percentage of the web page width, click the In Percent option button. Then enter a value in the text box.

6 Click OK.

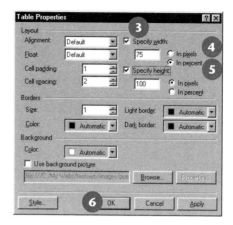

Changing Cell Width and Layout

Just as you can change the layout of an entire table, you can also change the layout of individual cells in a table. To fit a large amount of information into a single cell, for example, you can increase the width of the cell. You can right-align numbers in cells and left-align or center textual content. You can also create column and row headers to describe the labels and values included in your table.

TIP

Think about your other cells. *Consider the number of columns in your table as you set the cell width. For example, if you have two columns, you might want each column to take up half or slightly less than half of the web page's width.*

Change the Width and Alignment of a Cell

1. Right-click the cell.

2. Choose Cell Properties from the shortcut menu.

3. Select the horizontal alignment for the cell's contents—Left, Center, or Right—from the Horizontal Alignment drop-down list box.

4. Select the vertical alignment for the cell's contents—Top, Middle, Baseline, or Bottom—from the Vertical Alignment drop-down list box.

5. Select the Specify Width check box, and enter a value in the text box.

6. Click OK.

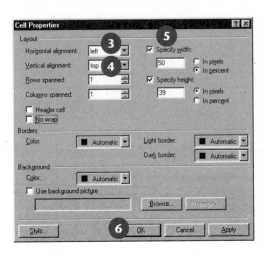

TRY THIS

Multiple header cells. *To create a row of header cells, click a cell in the row, choose Select from the Table menu and Row from the submenu, and then complete the steps for "Create a Header Cell." To create a column of header cells, click a cell in the column, choose Select Column from the Table menu, and then complete the steps for "Create a Header Cell."*

Create a Header Cell

1 Right-click the cell.

2 Choose Cell Properties from the shortcut menu.

3 Select the Header Cell check box.

4 To specify that cell contents shouldn't wrap—or shouldn't break onto separate lines—select the No Wrap check box.

5 Click OK.

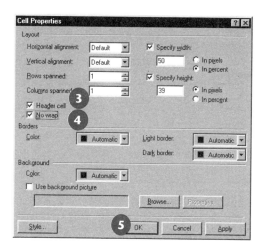

Changing a Cell's Background

Changing the background color of individual cells can be used to good effect in your tables. You could, for example, choose a brightly colored background for a single cell to draw attention to it.

Color the Cell Background

1. Right-click the cell.

2. Choose Cell Properties from the shortcut menu.

3. Select a color from the Background Color drop-down list box.

4. Click OK.

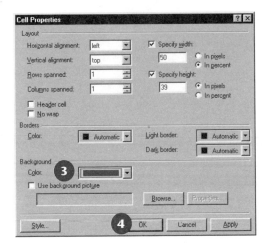

Use an Image for the Cell Background

1. Right-click the cell.

2. Choose Cell Properties from the shortcut menu.

3. Select the Use Background Picture check box.

4. Click Browse.

5. Select the image you want to use from the Select Background Image dialog box.

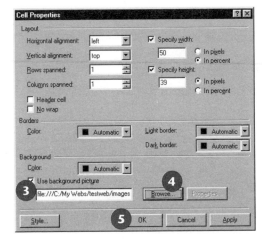

Changing Cell Border Colors

As with coloring the borders of an entire table, you have two options for recoloring the borders of a single cell. You can color all sides of the cell with the same color, or you can choose two colors to give the cell a shadow effect.

TIP

Cell properties take precedence. *The Cell Properties dialog box's border settings override the Table Properties dialog box's border settings.*

Color the Cell Border with One Color

1 Right-click the cell.

2 Choose Cell Properties from the shortcut menu.

3 Select a color for the cell's border from the Borders Color drop-down list box.

4 Click OK.

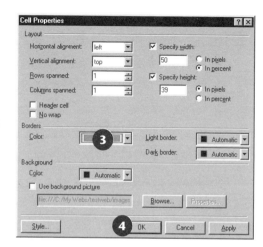

Color the Cell Border with Different Colors

1 Right-click the cell.

2 Choose Cell Properties from the shortcut menu.

3 Select a color for the cell's bottom and right borders from the Light Border drop-down list box.

4 Select a color for the cell's top and left borders from the Dark Border drop-down list box.

5 Click OK.

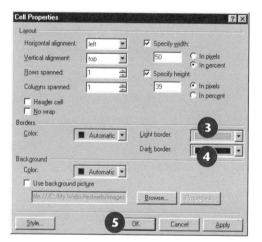

6

Changing Cell Span

If the information in one cell applies to several cells in a row or column (as is often the case with header cells), you might want to stretch the cell to span the row or column rather than retyping the same information in each cell. By doing so, you not only save yourself time but also simplify your table.

TIP

Normal span is one row.
Typically, a cell spans, or occupies, a single row or single column of a table.

Stretch the Cell to Span Multiple Rows

1 Right-click the cell.

2 Choose Cell Properties from the shortcut menu.

3 Specify how many rows and columns this cell should span in the Rows Spanned and Columns Spanned boxes.

4 Click OK.

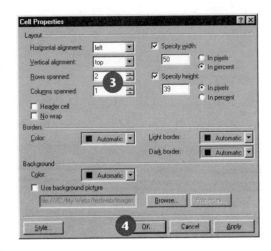

7

Working with Frames

Frames pages let you divide a web browser window into a set of "window panes," or frames, and thereby give you the ability to show more than one HTML document at a time. For example, you might use one frame to show your web site's table of contents while using another frame to show the different web pages requested by the web site visitor.

To create a frames page, you describe a grid of frames that you want a web browser to display. Then for each frame, you provide a hyperlink to the HTML document—the actual web page—which the web browser should display in that frame.

The frames page itself is just another HTML document. To display a frames page, a visitor simply clicks a hyperlink to the frames page. Or a visitor can indirectly request the frames page, such as by visiting a web site for which the frames page is the home page. Once a visitor requests (either directly or indirectly) to load a frames page, the web server passes the frames page to the visitor's web browser and then passes the individual HTML documents—the target frames—that will fill the frames of the frames page.

Creating Frames Pages

You can create a frames page by choosing a frames page template from the New dialog box. FrontPage includes a rich variety of frames pages to choose from. Once you have created the frames page, you can then specify which web pages go in the frames.

TIP

Use the No Frames tab. *Click the No Frames tab to edit the page visitors with browsers that don't support frames will see when they come to your site.*

Create a Frames Page

1. Choose New from the File menu and Page from the submenu.

2. Click the Frames Pages tab.

3. Select a template from the list box.

4. Click OK.

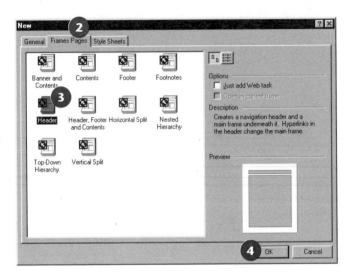

Add a New Page to a Frame

1. Open the frames page.

2. Click a frame.

3. Click New Page.

4. Add text, images, and hyperlinks to the new page.

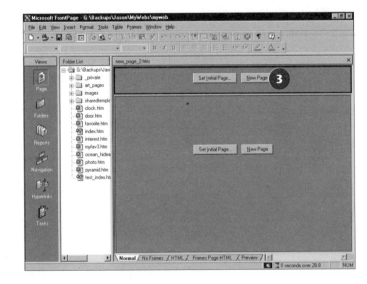

TIP

Use a page not in your web site. *Click the Select A File On Your Computer button in the Create Hyperlink dialog box to browse your computer for the initial page. Click the Use Your Web Page To Select A Page Or File button to choose a page on the Internet.*

Add an Existing Page to a Frame

1. Open the frames page.

2. Click a frame.

3. Click Set Initial Page.

4. Select the page you want to add.

5. Click OK.

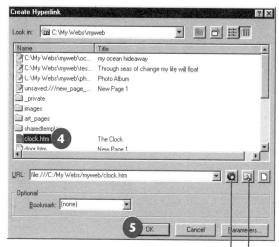

Click here to find a page on the web.

Click here to find a page on your computer.

Saving Pages in a Frames Page

If you add new pages to a frames page, you can save them by using the Save Page As command on the Frames menu. This command works in the same basic way as the Save As command on the File menu.

TIP

Title vs. filename. *The name that you enter in the File Name box becomes the filename of the HTML document. Click Change to set the title that appears at the top of the web browser window when the frames page is displayed.*

Save a Page

1. Click in the frame containing the page you want to save.

2. Choose Save Page As from the Frames menu.

3. Type a name for the page in the File Name text box.

4. Click Change, and type a title for the page in the Title text box.

5. Click Save.

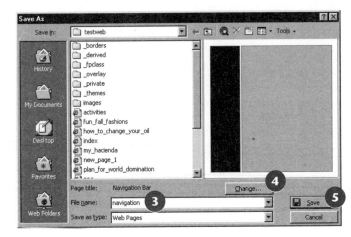

Splitting and Deleting Frames

If the frames page that you initially create doesn't work or look the way you want, you can easily split frames into still more frames. You can also delete frames.

Split a Frame

1. Click the frame to select it.

2. Choose Split Frame from the Frames menu.

3. Click an option button to split the selected frame vertically into columns or horizontally into rows.

4. Click OK.

Delete a Frame

1. Click the frame to select it.

2. Choose Delete Frame from the Frames menu.

Editing Frames Pages

You can edit a frames page even after you create it. For example, you can adjust or resize the frames page's grid. You can rename the frames page or change its URL. And, of course, you can create and edit the individual pages that are displayed in the frames page's frames.

SEE ALSO

See "Entering Text in a Page" on page 36 for information on adding text to a web page, "Inserting Images" on page 62 for information on adding images to a web page, and "Creating Hyperlinks" on page 38 for information on adding hyperlinks to a web page.

TIP

Use pixels. *FrontPage calibrates frame margin width in pixels.*

Edit a Page in a Frames Page

1. Open the frames page with the page you want to edit.

2. Edit the page directly in the frame, or select the page and choose Open Page In New Window from the Frames menu.

3. Add text, images, and hyperlinks to the page in the usual way.

Change the Frames Page Grid

1. Open the frames page you want to change.

2. Resize the dimensions of the individual frames in the grid by dragging the gridlines.

3. Split a frame by holding down the Ctrl key and then dragging the frame gridline.

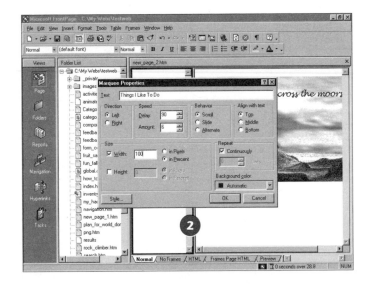

Edit frames page properties.
*Click the Frames Page button
on the Frame Properties
window to edit the properties
of the frames page, the page
that holds the individual
frames.*

Edit the Frame Properties

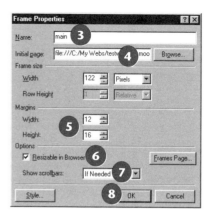

1 Open the frames page with the frame you want to edit.

2 Right-click the frame, and choose Frame Properties from the shortcut menu.

3 Type a new name or edit the existing name for the frame in the Name text box.

4 Type a new URL or edit the existing URL for the frame in the Initial Page text box. Or click Browse, and then use the dialog box to select an HTML document.

5 Adjust the frame margins in the Margins Width and Height boxes.

6 Clear the Resizable In Browser check box if you don't want web site visitors to resize the frames page's frames as they view them.

7 Select an entry from the Show Scrollbars drop-down list box to indicate whether a browser should provide scroll bars for the frame.

8 Click OK.

Specifying Target Frames

You can control what happens to a visitor's web browser window after clicking a hyperlink inside a frame. Specifically, you can control whether the new HTML document appears in the same frame, a new frame, or a new window.

TIP

Target the same frame.
If you want the target of a hyperlink to appear in the same frame as the page containing the hyperlink, select the Same Frame entry from the Common Targets list box.

TIP

Specify a target for a form.
You can specify a target frame for a form in the same way you specify a target frame from a page.

Specify a Target Frame for a Page

1. Right-click a frame.

2. Choose Frame Properties from the shortcut menu.

3. Click Frames Page.

4. Click the General tab.

5. Click the Default Target Frame button.

6. Select a target frame from the Common Targets list box.

7. Click OK.

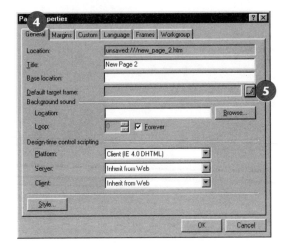

8

Inserting FrontPage Components

FrontPage Components represent a key feature of Microsoft FrontPage. People with little or no background in computer programming can use FrontPage Components to create interactive web sites and web sites that automatically update. FrontPage Components automate such tasks as displaying how many viewers have visited your web site and changing graphics images or references to HTML files on a certain date. Sophisticated FrontPage Components in form pages (described in the next section) tell the server to redisplay the information a web site visitor just entered, and simple components perform rudimentary tasks, such as inserting the designated content. Some FrontPage Components are static and wait for user input. (The Confirmation Field works this way.) Other components are dynamic and change automatically each time a visitor requests the page. (The Hit Counter works this way.)

FrontPage can also work with Microsoft Office Web Components, which you can use to insert interactive spreadsheets, charts, and graphs into your web pages.

Even if you haven't added any FrontPage Components on your own, your FrontPage web probably already includes some. If, for example, you created your web site using one of FrontPage's web wizards, FrontPage added several components for you as it created the site. You can recognize most of the FrontPage Components on your web pages by the robot icon that appears when you run your mouse over the component.

How FrontPage
Components Work

In essence, FrontPage Components provide special instructions to the web server software, and sometimes web browser software—instructions that go beyond those typically included as part of the standard HTML instructions that comprise a standard web page. Not every web server understands these special instructions, however. All FrontPage-generated FrontPage Components that reside on a web server, such as the Hit Counter search form, work only on web servers that have either the FrontPage Personal Web Server installed (as might be the case in a small intranet) or FrontPage Server Extensions installed (as might be the case on a large intranet or on an Internet server.)

These special instructions created by the FrontPage Component are called SmartHTML. For example, when you include the Hit Counter in your web page, the following SmartHTML code is generated:

If a web page with this SmartHTML code is displayed by a web server that can correctly interpret the code—for example, a web server with FrontPage Server Extensions—the web server returns a standard HTML page but substitutes the number of hits in place of the SmartHTML.

```
<p><!--webbot bot="HitCounter" u-custom b-reset="FALSE" i-digits="0" i-image="0"
PREVIEW="&lt;strong&gt;[Hit Counter]&lt;/strong&gt;" i-resetvalue="0" -->
</p>
```

Working with FrontPage Components

A few tasks apply to all of the FrontPage Components you can create. For example, you can access the FrontPage Component's Properties dialog box in the same manner. All FrontPage Components also create HTML code, which you can view and edit as you would the rest of the HTML code on a web page. You can also delete FrontPage Components in exactly the same way.

TIP

Undo. *To restore a deleted FrontPage Component, click the Undo toolbar button.*

Change Component Properties

1 Open the web page with the FrontPage Component.

2 Double-click the FrontPage Component.

3 Make your changes and click OK.

View the HTML Code Created by a FrontPage Component

1 Open the web page with the FrontPage Component.

2 Click the HTML tab in FrontPage.

3 Click the Normal tab to resume editing the web page.

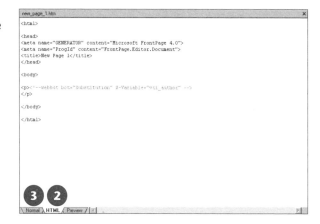

Delete a FrontPage Component

1 Open the web page with the FrontPage Component you want to delete.

2 Select the component you want to delete by clicking it.

3 Press the Delete key.

Inserting Hit Counters

Hit Counters are a very popular feature of many web pages. They let both web site visitors and web site creators easily see how much traffic a web page is getting.

You are visitor 013

Insert a Hit Counter

1. Open the web page in which you want to place the Hit Counter (most likely the home page of your web).

2. Click to place the cursor where you want to add the Hit Counter, and click the Insert Component toolbar button.

3. Choose Hit Counter from the drop-down menu.

4. Select a look for the Hit Counter by clicking one of the Counter Style option buttons.

5. Select the Fixed Number Of Digits check box if you want to fix your counter size at a certain number of digits.

6. Click OK.

Adding an Advertising Banner

Many web sites earn the money they need to stay in business by selling space on advertising banners—the banners that run across web pages with ads for different companies. FrontPage provides a component that makes it easy to create these necessary devices.

TIP

Change the image order. *Use the Move Up and Move Down buttons to change the order of the advertisements.*

TIP

Match image sizes. *The banner ad works best if you use images that are approximately the same size.*

Insert a Banner Ad

1 Open the web page in which you want to insert a banner ad.

2 Place the cursor where you want to insert the banner.

3 Click the Insert Component toolbar button, and choose Banner Ad Manager from the drop-down menu.

4 Specify the banner's width and height.

5 Select a transition effect from the Transition Effect drop-down list box.

6 Specify how long each advertisement should display.

7 Enter the advertising company's home page, if appropriate.

8 Click Add to insert the ad images.

9 Click OK.

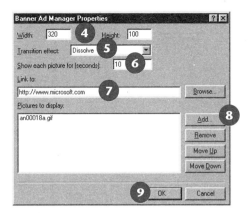

Inserting Animated Buttons

You can use FrontPage to create animated hover buttons that come alive when a visitor moves the mouse over it. Hover buttons can add to a feeling of interactivity on a web page or just give a page a little pizzazz.

TIP

Resize a button. *Make sure the button is large enough to hold the text you entered in the Button Text box. If it isn't, right-click the hover button and choose Hover Button Properties from the shortcut menu to change the hover button's size.*

Insert a Hover Button

1. Open the web page in which you want to insert a hover button.

2. Place the cursor where you want to insert the button.

3. Choose Component from the Insert menu and Hover Button from the submenu.

4. Enter the button text.

5. Enter the page that you want displayed when a visitor clicks the hover button, or click Browse to locate the page.

6. Select a color from the Button Color drop-down list box.

7. Select an animation effect from the Effect drop-down list box. Then select the color of the effect.

8. Click OK.

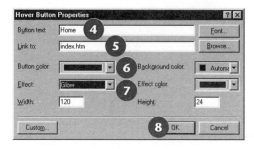

Inserting a Table of Contents

A table of contents creates an outline of hyperlinks to each page in your web site. Visitors to your web site can use the table of contents to navigate through the web site. You can also configure the table of contents so that it updates itself whenever you add, delete, or rename a page.

TIP

Use your home page. *If you want a list of all the web pages in your web site, assign your home page as the starting point for the table of contents.*

TIP

Manual recompute. *Very large web sites will take a long time to recompute when the Recompute Table Of Contents check box is selected. If you don't select this option, recompute the table of contents by opening the page with the table of contents and then saving the page.*

Insert a Table of Contents

1 Open the web page in which you want to place the table of contents.

2 Click the Insert Component toolbar button, and choose Table Of Contents from the drop-down menu.

3 Type the URL for the first web page you want to include in the table of contents.

4 Select a heading font size from the Heading Font Size drop-down list box.

5 Select the Show Each Page Only Once check box to list a web page only once in the table of contents.

6 Select the Show Pages With No Incoming Hyperlinks check box to display all pages on the site.

7 Select the Recompute Table Of Contents When Any Other Page Is Edited check box to ensure that any changes you make to the web site are reflected in an updated table of contents.

8 Click OK.

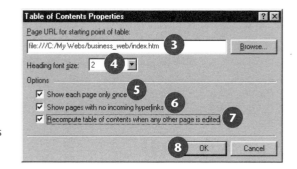

8

Creating Marquees

Another way you can add visual interest to your web pages is by creating marquees. Marquees use moving text for emphasis—the same way that some movie theaters use a marquee to tell you what movie is playing and who's starring.

TIP

Set the marquee's style.
Click Style, and use the tabs in the Style dialog box to specify the marquee's font, border, and background image.

Create a Marquee

1. Open the web page in which you want to add a marquee.

2. Click the line on which you want to place the marquee.

3. Click the Insert Component toolbar button, and select Marquee from the drop-down menu.

4. Type the marquee text you want to roll onto and off of the web page in the Text box.

5. Click OK.

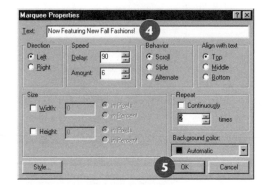

Internet Explorer only.
*Marquees do not display in
browsers other than Microsoft
Internet Explorer. People using
Netscape Navigator or other
browsers will still be able to
see your heading if you decide
to convert it into a marquee
because a normal line of text
will substitute for any
marquees you create.*

Convert an Existing Heading to a Marquee

1 Open the web page in which you want to add a marquee.

2 Select the heading you want to be a marquee.

3 Click the Insert Component toolbar button, and select Marquee from the drop-down menu.

4 Click OK.

The text you selected appears here.

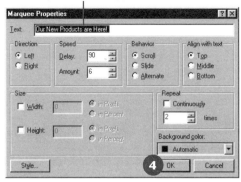

8

Customizing Marquees

After you have created a marquee, the next step is to customize the marquee to fit the page and to suit your own tastes as well. FrontPage offers several ways in which you can customize a marquee. You can change the direction and speed at which it scrolls across the screen. You can also specify the marquee's size and background color.

TIP

Smoother marquees. *Set the Delay to a smaller number to make the marquee move smoothly. Set the Delay and Amount to a large number to make the text "hop" across the screen in an abrupt motion.*

Change the Marquee's Properties

1. Right-click the marquee.

2. Choose Marquee Properties from the shortcut menu.

3. Edit the text shown in the Text box.

4. Click a Direction option button to indicate the direction in which the marquee should move.

5. Specify the speed of the marquee in the Speed boxes.

   ◆ Delay specifies how long the text pauses between each move across the page.

   ◆ Amount specifies how far the text should move after each delay.

6. Click a Behavior option button to indicate the kind of marquee you want.

   ◆ Scroll lets the marquee roll onto and off of the web page.

   ◆ Slide lets the marquee roll onto the web page and then stop.

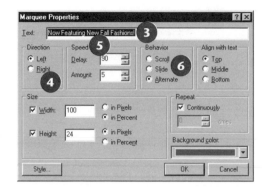

Resize with your mouse. *You can also change the width or height of a marquee by clicking it (to select it) and then dragging one of its selection handles.*

Continuous marquees. *Select the Continuously check box to have a scrolling or alternating marquee run as long as the web page is open. Or clear the check box, and enter the number of times you want the marquee to run in the Times box.*

Remove a marquee. *To delete a marquee, click it and press the Delete key.*

Background color overrides transparency. *Before you set a background color, the marquee text appears to float over your web page. Setting a background color creates a colored box that the text moves in.*

◆ Alternate lets the marquee roll onto and off of the web page from different directions.

7 Select the Width check box, and then set the width and specify the unit of measurement you're using.

8 Select the Height check box, and then set the height and specify the unit of measurement you're using.

9 Select a background color from the Background Color drop-down list box.

10 Click OK.

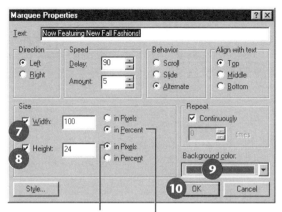

Selecting the In Pixels option specifies the width or height in number of pixels.

Selecting the In Percent option specifies the width or height as a percentage of the web page width or height.

8

Inserting Substitution Components

You use Substitution Components to display parameters on a web page. Parameters include such bits of information as the web site author, a page's description, the name of the person who last modified the web site page, and other user-defined configuration variables.

SEE ALSO

See "Working with Parameters" on page 184 for more information about creating and editing parameters.

TIP

Make a Substitution Component work. *In order for the Substitution Component to work, you must supply values for each of the variables listed in the Substitute With drop-down list box. To do this, choose Web Settings from the Tools menu, click Add on the Parameters tab, and then supply the values.*

Insert the Substitution Component

1. Open the web page in which you want to place the Substitution Component.

2. Click the Insert Component toolbar button, and choose Substitution from the drop-down menu.

3. Select a substitution variable from the Substitute With drop-down list box.

4. Click OK.

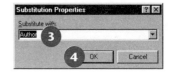

Confirming Visitor Input

You use confirmation fields on Confirmation Form Pages to verify the information a visitor has provided. In order for a confirmation field to work, you must have a form created for collecting information and a confirmation form attached to that form.

SEE ALSO

See "Creating a Confirmation Form Page" on page 171 for more information about creating a Confirmation Form Page.

TIP

Form field names. *You must enter the form field name exactly as you have named it on the form. If you can't remember the field's name, right-click it and choose Form Field Properties from the shortcut menu. Select the name, right-click it, and choose Copy from the shortcut menu. Then, in the Confirmation Field Component, right-click and choose Paste from the shortcut menu.*

Insert a Confirmation Field

① Open the Confirmation Form web page to which you want to add the Confirmation Field.

② Click to place the cursor where you want to add the confirmation field, and click the Insert Component toolbar button.

③ Select Confirmation Field from the list box, and click OK.

④ In the Confirmation Field Properties dialog box, enter the name of the form field you want to confirm and click OK.

8

Inserting Include Page Components

To simplify the tasks of maintaining your web site and keeping it up to date, you may want FrontPage to change some of the information on your web pages automatically. The Include Page Component serves this purpose by inserting the web page you specify at the location you select.

Insert the Include Page Component

1 Open the web page in which you want to place the Include Page Component.

2 Click the Insert Component toolbar button, and choose Include Page from the drop-down menu.

3 Type the URL address for the web page you want to include, or click Browse to browse the current web for the page.

4 Click OK.

Inserting Scheduled Pictures

You use Scheduled Pictures when you want to display particular images for a specific amount of time, for example, for selected months or seasons. You might also use Scheduled Pictures to illustrate sales promotions or limited-time offers.

TIP

Edit a Scheduled Picture. *You can't add a border or change the image type or alignment of a Scheduled Picture. However, you can link or unlink the image by using the Hyperlink or Unlink commands on the Edit menu.*

TIP

Expired images. *If the Scheduled Picture expiration date passes and you have not supplied an optional image, the Expired Scheduled Picture message appears in place of the image.*

Insert a Scheduled Picture

1. Open the web page in which you want to place the Scheduled Picture.

2. Click the Insert Component toolbar button, and choose Scheduled Picture from the drop-down menu.

3. Type the name of the image you want to include in the web page, or click Browse to display the Current Web dialog box, and select an image from the list box.

4. Enter the date and time the image should start appearing in the web page.

5. Enter the date and time the image should stop appearing in the web page.

6. Supply an optional image that should appear before or after the original image appears.

7. Click OK.

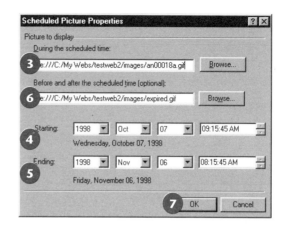

Inserting Scheduled Include Pages

Just as you would use Scheduled Pictures to display images for a specific amount of time, you use the Scheduled Include Page Component to display an entire page of content for a specific amount of time. For example, you would use a Scheduled Include Page if you wanted to regularly update a web site by substituting new web pages. With Scheduled Include Pages, the links automatically change when the time period expires, so you have to work only with the individual pages of included content.

TIP

Make a page private. *If you don't want the page that you are including in the Scheduled Include Page to be directly viewable, you can store the page in the _private folder.*

Insert the Scheduled Include Page Component

1. Open the web page in which you want to place the Scheduled Include Page Component.

2. Click the Insert Component toolbar button, and choose Scheduled Include Page from the drop-down menu.

3. Type the URL for the web page you want to include.

4. Enter the date and time the web page should start appearing.

5. Enter the date and time the web page should stop appearing.

6. Optionally, supply the URL for another web page that should appear before or after the scheduled web page appears.

7. Click OK.

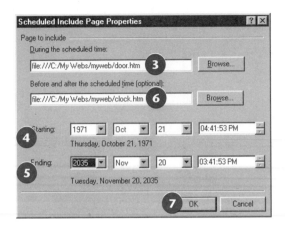

Inserting Categories

Categories are a powerful new workgroup feature that makes it easier for a webmaster to include pages that other people have created. A webmaster creates a page that links to all pages in a certain category, and then when a person creates a web page that they specify as belonging to that category, FrontPage automatically creates a new link to it.

Insert the Categories Component

1 Open the web page in which you want to place the Category Component.

2 Place the cursor where you want to add the list of pages.

3 Click the Insert Component toolbar button, and choose Categories from the drop-down menu.

4 Select categories from the list box to include on the page.

5 Select an entry from the Sort Pages By drop-down list box to specify how you want the pages sorted.

6 Specify any additional information that should be included with the pages.

7 Click OK.

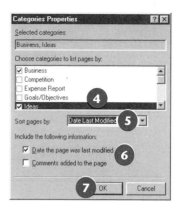

8

Inserting a Search Form

Search forms are valuable tools that can help visitors find the information they want quickly and easily. FrontPage allows you to easily add a search form to your web site so that visitors can search the pages on your site.

Insert a Search Form

1. Open the web page in which you want to place the Search Form.

2. Place the cursor where you want to add the list of pages.

3. Click the Insert Component toolbar button, and choose Search Form from the drop-down menu.

4. Type a label for the search form.

5. Specify how wide you want the text box for the search form to be.

6. Type a label for the "Start Search" button.

7. Type a label for the "Clear" button.

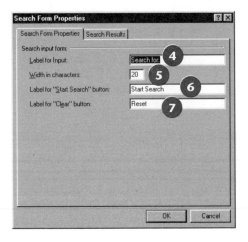

TIP

Search pages. *To create an entire search page, choose New from the File menu and Page from the submenu. Select Search Page from the list of templates to create a new page with a search form already set up.*

⑧ Click the Search Results tab.

⑨ Select formats from the drop-down list boxes to specify how you want web pages' dates and times displayed.

⑩ Select the Display Score check box to display how closely the search results match.

⑪ Select the Display File Date and Display File Size check boxes to display the file date and size.

⑫ Click OK.

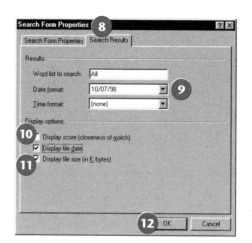

This is the finished search form.

Microsoft Office Web Components

Microsoft Office 2000 includes three small ActiveX components called Office Web Components that users of Microsoft Excel and Microsoft Access can use to create web pages that permit users to directly interact with data in their web browsers. Large companies can use these components to give their employees access to data so they can examine and make changes to it remotely. Individuals and companies that want to publish data to a web site in a more interactive manner can also use the Office Web Components to permit visitors to examine and manipulate data on their own.

To interact with data using a Microsoft Office Web Component, visitors need to use Internet Explorer 4.01 or later and have a license for Microsoft Office 2000.

To create a web page containing interactive data, it is best to use the Save As Web Page feature in Excel 2000 and Access 2000 to create the page. Creating the page with Excel or Access will make linking the Office Web Component to the desired data source much easier. You can then use FrontPage to perform any necessary editing and linking of the web page.

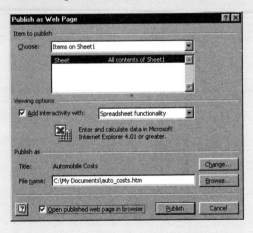

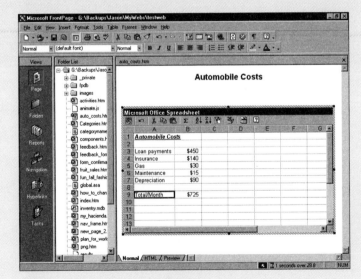

Inserting Office Components

Most of the time, you create Office components in Microsoft Excel or Access, but occasionally you need to insert them in a web page yourself. Although it usually works better to do this from the program in which you or your company created the data, FrontPage does allow you to manually insert Microsoft Office Web Components.

TIP

Create an Office chart. *After inserting an Office spreadsheet on a page, you can create an Office chart based on it by clicking the Insert Component toolbar button, choosing Office Chart from the drop-down menu, and then using the Microsoft Office Chart Wizard.*

Insert an Office Web Component

1 Open the page in which you want to place the Office Web Component.

2 Click the Insert Component toolbar button, and then choose an Office Web Component from the drop-down menu.

3 To connect Office Spreadsheet or Office PivotTable to a data source, click the Property Toolbox toolbar button in the component.

4 Choose either the Import Data tab or the Data Source tab, depending on which component you're using.

5 Enter the location of your data source and any necessary parameters.

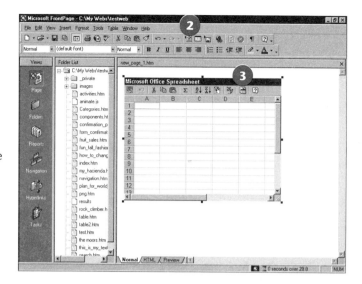

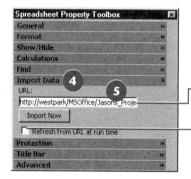

Type the location of your data here.

Select this check box to have your data updated every time the component loads.

Working with Code

Code is the set of programming instructions that underlies all web pages and all the programs that run inside web pages. Using code gives you precise control over your web pages and programs. However, working with code can be very intimidating to users who are not experienced with programming or working with scripts. On the other hand, not being able to work with code can be frustrating for those users who know and love coding pages by hand. FrontPage satisfies both types of user by shielding the underlying code, which streamlines page-creation time, while at the same time providing quick access to the code as well as making it easier to work with.

As a user of FrontPage, you never have to work with code. However, if you want to delve a little deeper into the mechanics of web-page creation, FrontPage provides a wealth of tools for you to use to create, modify, and insert code into your web pages. In the following sections, I briefly describe a few of these tools and explain how you can get started with them.

Working with HTML Code

You can work with the HTML code for a web page by clicking the HTML tab when you are in Page view. FrontPage color-codes HTML for you, making it easier to work with. FrontPage 2000 preserves the changes you make in the HTML tab, allowing you to format code to

exact specifications. You can also use FrontPage tools to make working with HTML easier. For example, if you want to create a table in the HTML tab, simply click the Table toolbar button, select a size for your table, and FrontPage will insert the proper code in your page.

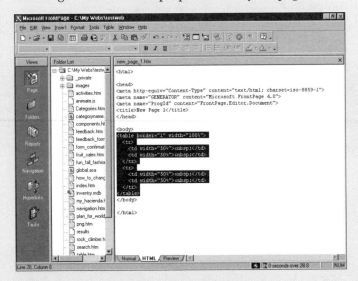

Working with Java Applets

You can insert any Java applets you've created into a web page in FrontPage by choosing Advanced from the Insert menu and Java Applet from the submenu. Enter the location of the applet, and modify any parameters you want.

Working with ActiveX Controls

You can insert any ActiveX control you have on your system by choosing Advanced from the Insert menu and ActiveX Control from the submenu. Select the control you want to add from the list, and then click OK. Double-click the inserted control to modify its properties.

Working with Visual Basic and Scripts

FrontPage comes with Microsoft Visual Basic Editor as well as Microsoft Script Editor, a tool you can use to work with JavaScript, VBScript, and ActiveX components. These tools are both very powerful, but you need to know about programming in order to use them effectively. To access them, choose Macro from the Tools menu and then choose either Visual Basic Editor or Microsoft Script Editor from the submenu.

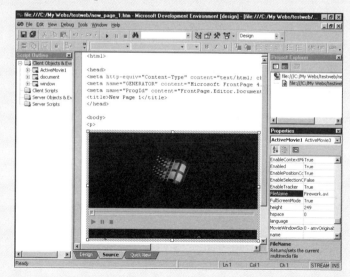

Working with Forms

Forms let you collect information from site visitors. To use a form, a visitor simply types information in the form's fields, clicks a button that submits the information to the web site server, and then the server collects and processes the information according to the instructions of the form's handler.

All Microsoft FrontPage forms have several basic elements:

- ◆ Questions or requests for information
- ◆ Fields in which visitors type information
- ◆ Submit and Reset buttons that let the visitor control whether he or she submits or clears the form
- ◆ Form handlers associated with the form that control what happens to the visitor's input

It's important to note that FrontPage doesn't require you to create computer-programming scripts in order to use forms or handle the form data. (This is the usual case when including forms in a web site.) FrontPage creates the scripts that handle the forms automatically. However, your web server does need to support FrontPage Server Extensions.

Creating Forms from Templates

You create feedback and user registration forms to gather various types of information from visitors. Use a feedback form to collect feedback about your site, services, or products. Use a user registration form so that visitors can register themselves to access a web site.

Create a Feedback Form

1. Choose New from the File menu and Page from the submenu.

2. Select Feedback Form from the list box.

3. Click OK.

4. Customize the text, comments, or fields of the form.

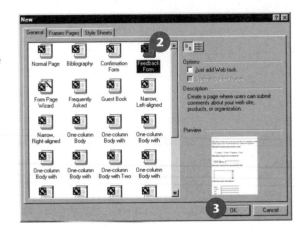

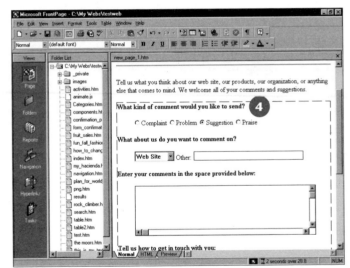

TIP

Where results go. *By default, FrontPage saves feedback form data to a text file on the web server using the Save Results form handler.*

Create a User Registration Page

1 Choose New from the File menu and Page from the submenu.

2 Select User Registration from the list box.

3 Click OK.

4 Customize the text, comments, and fields of the form.

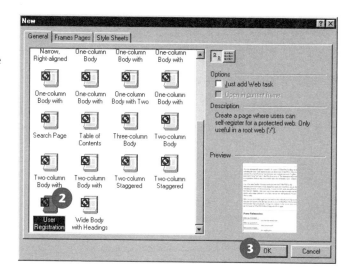

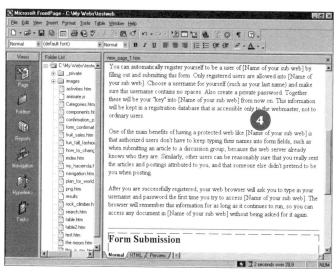

Using the Form Page Wizard

The Form Page Wizard speeds up the creation of forms and provides form templates for certain types of forms you might want to use repeatedly. The wizard not only creates a form for you but also attaches the proper form handler to the form.

Create a Form Using the Form Page Wizard

1 Choose New from the File menu and Page from the submenu.

2 Select Form Page Wizard from the list box. Click OK, and then click Next.

3 Click Add to create a new question for your form.

4 Select the type of information you'll collect with this form from the list box. Click Next.

5 Set the options for the question you selected, give the variable a name, and then click Next.

6 Click Add to create additional questions, or click Next to move on.

7 Select the presentation options you want, and then click Next.

8 Select the output options you want, name the results file, and then click Next.

9 Click Finish.

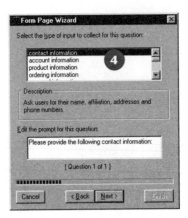

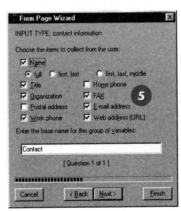

The Parts of a Form

You can use a variety of buttons and boxes on the forms that you create.

Radio buttons

Use radio buttons to let visitors choose from sets of mutually exclusive answers.

Drop-down menus

Use drop-down menus to let visitors choose one or more entries from a list of options.

Scrolling text box

Use a scrolling text box when you can't estimate how much room visitors will need or what structure or form visitors will use for entering information.

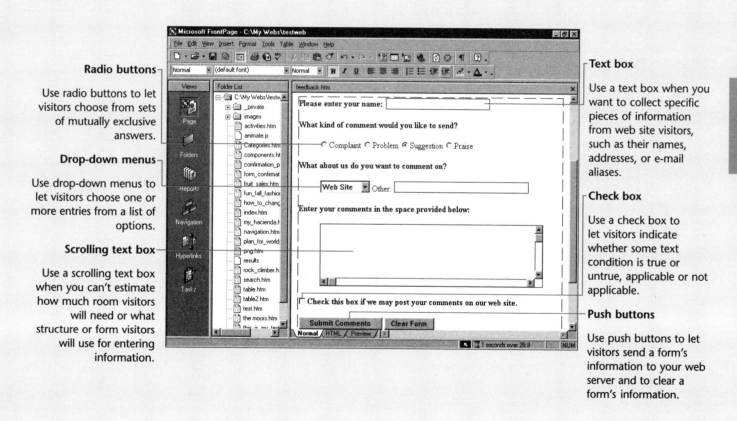

Text box

Use a text box when you want to collect specific pieces of information from web site visitors, such as their names, addresses, or e-mail aliases.

Check box

Use a check box to let visitors indicate whether some text condition is true or untrue, applicable or not applicable.

Push buttons

Use push buttons to let visitors send a form's information to your web server and to clear a form's information.

9

Inserting One-Line Text Boxes

FrontPage provides a variety of methods to create new forms or add new form elements to a page. Which method you choose depends on what you're already doing and what you want to do next. You use one-line text boxes to collect responses to short-answer type questions. For example, you might use a one-line text box to ask for a person's name, address, or telephone number.

Organize your forms.
Organize your form fields logically so they can be filled in easily. For example, to collect name and address information with a form, arrange the fields so that a visitor can type his or her name first, then the street address, the city, and the zip code.

Insert a One-Line Text Box Field

1 Open the web page in which you want to place the One-Line Text Box field.

2 Choose Form from the Insert menu and One-Line Text Box from the submenu.

3 Click to place the cursor to the left of the One-Line Text Box field, and then type the field's title.

Constrain the Responses

1 Right-click the One-Line Text Box field, and choose Form Field Validation from the shortcut menu.

2 Optionally, constrain the allowable response content to text, integers, or numbers only.

3 Define the constraints using the Text Format boxes, the Numeric Format buttons, and the Data Length and Data Value boxes.

4 Click OK.

3 E-mail Address: [ ] Submit Reset

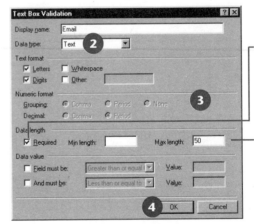

Select this check box to require a response in the One-Line Text Box field.

Describe the range of values numerically for numeric responses or alphabetically for textual responses.

Default text box values.
*Include an initial value in a
One-Line Text Box field only
when the majority of visitors
would respond to this question
with that value. For example, if
most of the people filling in a
State box would enter "CA" for
California, you might specify
this as the initial value.*

Hide passwords. *If you select
Yes for the Password Field
option, a web browser won't
display the actual characters
that someone types in the text
box. Instead, the web browser
will substitute the asterisk
character.*

Change the Properties of a One-Line Text Box Field

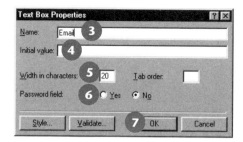

1 Right-click the One-Line Text Box field.

2 Choose Form Field Properties from the shortcut menu.

3 Type the name of the field in the Name text box.

4 Optionally, type the initial value you want inside the One-Line Text Box field in the Initial Value text box.

5 Optionally, change the width of the field in the Width In Characters box.

6 Optionally, click a Password Field option button.

7 Click OK.

Inserting Scrolling Text Boxes

Scrolling text boxes work much like one-line text boxes except they allow web site visitors to enter more information. If you choose not to constrain the length of visitors' inputs in scrolling text boxes, they can type several paragraphs.

TIP

Keep forms short. *As a general rule, you'll want to keep your forms short. Web visitors typically don't and won't spend more than a few minutes filling out an online form.*

TIP

Solicit comments. *A scrolling text box is best used for visitors to enter comments or special requests for information.*

Insert a Scrolling Text Box Field

1 Open the web page in which you want to place the Scrolling Text Box field.

2 Choose Form from the Insert menu and Scrolling Text Box from the submenu.

3 Click to place the cursor to the left of the Scrolling Text Box field.

4 Type the title for the Scrolling Text Box field.

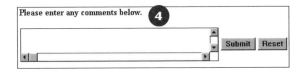

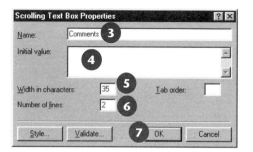

Suggest a response. *You can suggest a response to a Scrolling Text Box field by including an example response in the Initial Value text box.*

Form field validation. *You can change a scrolling text box's validation properties in the same way as you change the form field validation properties for a one-line text box.*

Tab order. *Many users press the Tab key after filling out a field to jump to the next field. If you want to specify the exact order in which users should move to fields after pressing the Tab key, enter a tab order in the Tab Order text box.*

Change the Properties of a Scrolling Text Box Field

1 Right-click the Scrolling Text Box field.

2 Choose Form Field Properties from the shortcut menu.

3 Type the name of the field in the Name text box.

4 Optionally, type the initial value you want inside the Scrolling Text Box field in the Initial Value text box.

5 Optionally, change the width of the field in the Width In Characters box.

6 Optionally, change the height of the field in the Number Of Lines box.

7 Click OK.

9

Inserting Check Boxes and Radio Buttons

Most forms include at least a few radio buttons (also called option buttons) or check boxes. You use radio buttons with multiple-choice type answers in which the choices are typically mutually exclusive. You use check boxes to ask visitors to mark all options that apply.

Insert a Check Box Field

1. Open the web page in which you want to place the Check Box field.

2. Choose Form from the Insert menu and Check Box from the submenu.

3. Click to place the cursor to the right of the Check Box field.

4. Type the title for the Check Box field.

☐ Please send me a catalog. **4**

Insert a Radio Button Field

1. Open the web page in which you want to place the Radio Button field.

2. Choose Form from the Insert menu and Radio Button from the submenu.

3. Click to place the cursor to the right of the Radio Button field.

4. Type the title for the Radio Button field.

How would you rate your expertise? **4**

○ Beginning ○ Intermediate ○ Advanced ⦿ I could teach you a lesson

Name a Radio Button or Check Box Field

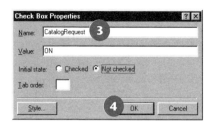

1 Right-click the Radio Button or Check Box field.

2 Choose Form Field Properties from the shortcut menu.

3 Type the name of the field in the Name text box.

4 Click OK.

Require a Response to a Radio Button Field

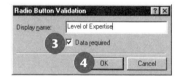

1 Right-click the Radio Button field.

2 Choose Form Field Validation from the shortcut menu.

3 Select the Data Required check box to require a response to the set of radio buttons.

4 Click OK.

9

Inserting Drop-Down Menu Fields

You use the Drop-Down Menu button on the Forms toolbar to create drop-down menus and list boxes for your forms. Drop-down menus and list boxes give web site visitors the opportunity to scroll through a list of possible responses and then pick the best answer or even several answers, depending on how you set up the fields. Drop-down menus work in a fashion similar to radio buttons, but they take up less room on the screen, making them more appropriate for long, detailed lists of options.

Insert a Drop-Down Menu Field

1. Open the web page in which you want to place the Drop-Down Menu field.

2. Choose Form from the Insert menu and Drop-Down Menu from the submenu.

3. Place the cursor next to the Drop-Down Menu field, and type the name of the Drop-Down Menu field.

Constrain Drop-Down Menu Field Responses

1. Right-click the Drop-Down Menu field, and choose Form Field Validation from the shortcut menu.

2. Select the Data Required check box if you want to require a response to the Drop-Down Menu field.

3. Select the Disallow First Choice check box if you want to use the first item as a line for providing instructions (such as "Please pick one of the following").

4. Click OK.

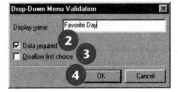

Add Choices to a Drop-Down Menu Field

1. Right-click the Drop-Down Menu field.

2. Choose Form Field Properties from the shortcut menu.

3. Type the name of the field in the Name text box.

4. Click Add.

5. Type the name of the first item you want listed in the Drop-Down Menu List field in the Choice text box.

6. Click the Selected option button under Initial State if you want the choice selected in the form.

7. Click OK.

8. Repeat steps 4 through 7 for each additional item you want to add to the drop-down menu.

9. Click OK.

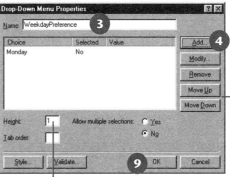

Click Move Up or Move Down to move the choice up or down in the drop-down menu.

Change the number of drop-down menu choices shown using the Height box.

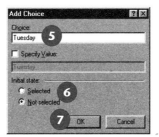

Inserting Push Buttons

In order for a form to function, visitors must have some way of submitting the form so that the responses can be gathered and processed by the form's handler. In this sense, push buttons play one of the most important roles in a form: they are the buttons that visitors use to tell the form handlers "Go!" When you insert these buttons in your forms, therefore, you need to make them visible and identifiable.

TIP

Rename buttons. *You can change the Submit Button field's label to any Value/Label you choose. Supply a new Value/Label to customize your form.*

Insert a Push Button Field

① Open the web page in which you want to place the Push Button field.

② Choose Form from the Insert menu and Push Button from the submenu.

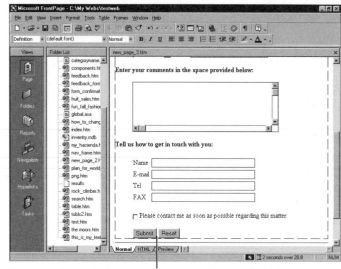

FrontPage inserts Submit and Reset push buttons by default when you insert a form field other than a Push Button field.

What push buttons do.
Clicking Submit tells the web browser to send the form's information to the web server. All forms need a Submit button of some sort. Clicking Reset tells the web browser to reset the form's buttons and boxes to their initial, or default, values. Clicking Normal tells the web browser to run the script, or program, you attach to the button.

Describe a Push Button Field

1. Right-click the Push Button field.

2. Choose Form Field Properties from the shortcut menu.

3. Type the name of the field in the Name text box.

4. Change the Value/Label of the Push Button field.

5. Optionally, change the type of button by clicking the Normal, Submit, or Reset option buttons.

6. Click OK.

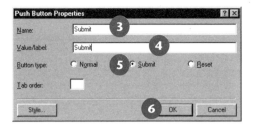

9

Inserting Picture Fields

To make your forms more interesting, you can also use images as form fields. For example, instead of using a text list to describe the products visitors can order over your web site, you can display a thumbnail graphic of each one. By doing so, you not only make your form more visually appealing but you also make it more informative. Visitors unfamiliar with your products can see exactly what you're offering before they place their orders.

Insert a Picture Field

1 Open the web page in which you want to place the Picture field.

2 Choose Form from the Insert menu and Picture from the submenu.

3 Select an image from the list box, or click Clip Art to use a clip art image.

4 Click OK.

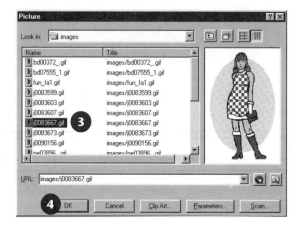

SEE ALSO

See "Adding Special Effects to Images" on page 78–79 for information on modifying images.

SEE ALSO

See "Positioning Images and Placing Text" on pages 68–69 for information on how to add text to your images.

Change the Properties of a Picture Field

1. Right-click the Picture field.

2. Choose Form Field Properties from the shortcut menu.

3. Type the name of the field in the Name text box.

4. Click the General tab.

5. Enter alternative representations in the Low-Res and Text text boxes.

6. Click OK.

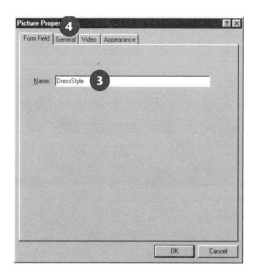

9

Adding Labels

Although you can type text anywhere you want inside a form, attaching field labels to the fields themselves is a more elegant and efficient solution to labeling. This makes it easier to keep fields together with the appropriate text.

TIP

Customize forms. *After you create an interactive web page, you customize the web page by editing the individual fields.*

TIP

Get the names right. *Make sure you enter all the field names exactly as they appear on your form. Select the field name in your form, and press Ctrl+C to copy it. In your Confirmation form, press Ctrl+V to paste it.*

Create a Label

1. Open the web page with the field to which you want to add a label.

2. Place the cursor next to the field, and type the text you want for the label.

3. Select the text and the field you want to label.

4. Choose Form from the Insert menu and Label from the submenu.

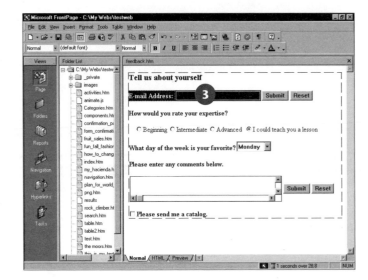

Creating a Confirmation Form Page

Use a Confirmation form to acknowledge a web visitor's input on a Feedback, Survey, or User Registration form. The form's fields redisplay the input so that the visitor can edit any information incorrectly entered.

Create a Confirmation Form Page

1 Choose New from the File menu and Page from the submenu.

2 Select Confirmation Form from the list box.

3 Click OK.

4 Customize the form fields by right-clicking them and choosing Confirmation Field Properties from the shortcut menu.

5 Enter a new field name to confirm.

6 Click OK.

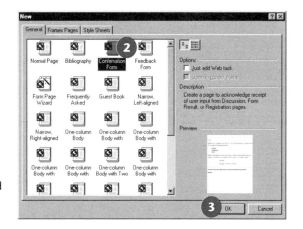

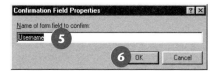

Attaching a Confirmation Form

Once you have a Confirmation form created, you can attach it to a form (for instance, a Survey or Feedback form) so that it appears whenever a visitor completes the form.

SEE ALSO

See "Confirming Visitor Input" on page 141 for more information on inserting Confirmation fields.

Attach a Confirmation Form to a Form Page

① Open the form page to which you want to attach the Confirmation form.

② Right-click the form.

③ Choose Form Properties from the shortcut menu.

④ Click Options.

⑤ Click the Confirmation Page tab.

⑥ Specify the Confirmation form you want displayed after the form page has been completed in the URL Of Confirmation Page text box. Or click Browse to locate the Confirmation form.

⑦ Click OK.

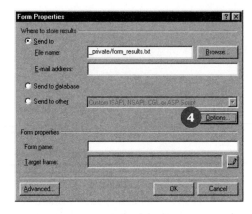

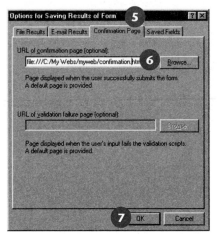

Saving Form Results

Once you have your form created, you need to specify what you want to do with the data the form collects. For Survey and Feedback forms, you use the Save Results form handler to tell the server what information you want to collect from visitors and how you want this information stored.

TIP

About form handlers. *A form handler is simply a program that runs on a web server. The form handler program runs whenever someone submits a form to it. The most common forms run the Save Results form handler.*

TIP

Test a form. *You'll want to test your form before placing it in your web site. Specifically, you want to verify that together the form and the form handler do whatever you want them to do—such as correctly collecting and storing the form information.*

Set Up a File for Form Results

1. Open the web page with the form.

2. Right-click the form area.

3. Choose Form Properties from the shortcut menu.

4. Click the Send To option button.

5. Enter the name of the file where you want to save the information that web site visitors enter in the form.

6. Optionally, if you want the form results sent to an e-mail address, enter the e-mail address.

7. Click Options.

8. Select the file format from the File Format drop-down list box.

9. Optionally, select the Include Field Names check box.

10. Optionally, click the Saved Fields tab and use the Additional Information To Save check boxes to collect and save additional information about your web site visitors.

11. Click OK.

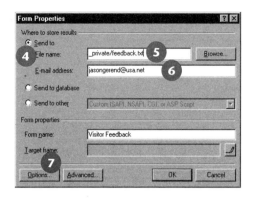

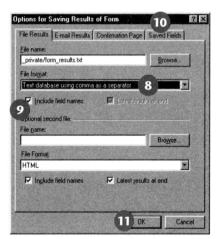

9

Forms, Privacy, and Passwords

When you create a form, you need to be very conscious of your web visitors' privacy and time. Presenting your visitors with a long, probing questionnaire is liable to result in no participation and no information. Your goal when you create a form is to obtain the information you need and nothing else. With that in mind, I'd like to present a few guidelines for developing forms.

Make the form to the point.

People are much more likely to fill out a form with only a few questions than a form with a larger number of questions, even if most of the fields on the longer form are optional. If you want people's opinions about your web page, present a few options, have an optional comments box, and make that the whole form.

Don't request more information than you need.

Many people are very wary of giving out information about themselves over the Internet and avoid filling out forms that ask any sort of personal information. Ask for only the information you need to fulfill the purpose of the form. Unless visitors request that you send them something, you don't need their addresses and phone numbers. If you're asking personal questions, don't ask for any contact information.

Don't password-protect your site.

Unless you charge for access to your web site, don't require visitors to become a member of your web site and pick a user name and password. Many people feel burdened by the need to remember user names and passwords and avoid web sites for which they need to register, even if they're free.

Use a secure site for sensitive information.

If you're asking for credit card information, or even personal information such as home addresses and phone numbers, make sure your web site has a secure connection. Even if you do have a secure web page for ordering products, make sure that you also provide an easy way for customers to place the order another way, such as by printing out the form and faxing it to your company.

Use as few required fields as possible.

Required fields are necessary on forms such as order forms on which the visitors are requesting something, but on many other types of forms, they aren't necessary. Often visitors may intentionally leave a field blank because they don't want to disclose the information you are requesting. By requiring fields, you increase your chances that instead of receiving a partially filled out form, you won't receive any form.

Setting Up a Second Save Results File

If you want the information you collect on a form stored in two different places, you need to set up a second Save Results file associated with the Save Results form handler. You might want to do this, for instance, if you want to post the results of a survey on a web page and save them in a file as well.

Set Up a Second Save Results File

1. Open the form page.

2. Right-click the form area.

3. Choose Form Properties from the shortcut menu.

4. Click Options.

5. Type the name of the second Save Results page or file in the File Name text box under Optional Second File.

6. Select the file format from the File Format drop-down list box.

7. Click OK.

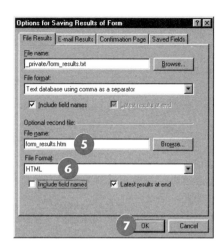

Restricting Web Access

If you create a User Registration page to allow only registered users to access a web site, visitors must supply a name and password in order to view the site. The Registration form handler handles the list of registered users and displays the form requiring visitors to enter a name and password.

SEE ALSO

See "Constrain the Responses" on page 158 for information on how to limit a user's input.

Set Up a List of Registered Users and Passwords

1 Open the User Registration page.

2 Right-click the form area.

3 Choose Form Properties from the shortcut menu.

4 Click Options.

5 Optionally, change the name of the web in the Web Name text box.

6 Optionally, change the name of the Username field in the Username Fields text box.

7 Optionally, change the name of the Password field in the Password Field text box.

8 Optionally, change the name of the Password Confirmation field in the Password Confirmation Field text box.

9 Optionally, change the URL of the web page you want to display when a visitor fails to register successfully in the URL Of Registration Failure Page text box.

10 Click OK.

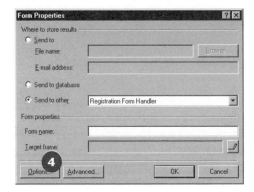

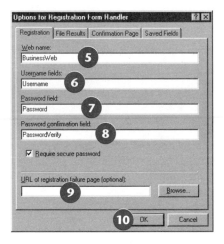

Change the Confirmation URL. *You can also change the Registration form's Confirmation URL by clicking the Confirmation tab and specifying the web page or form you want displayed after the Registration form has been completed.*

See "Attaching a Confirmation Form" on page 172 for more information on attaching Confirmation forms.

Change Registration Form Results

1. Open the User Registration page.

2. Right-click the form area.

3. Choose Form Properties from the shortcut menu.

4. Click Options.

5. Click the File Results tab.

6. Optionally, change the file used to store registration information in the File Name text box.

7. Optionally, select a file format for the results file from the File Format drop-down list box.

8. Optionally, click the Saved Fields tab and select Additional Information To Save check boxes to save the time, date, remote computer name, user name, or browser type to the results file.

9. Click OK.

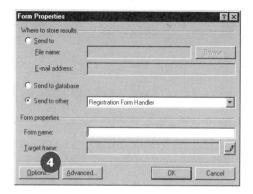

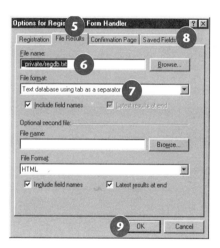

Setting Up a Database Connection

Databases are invaluable for storing and retrieving data. FrontPage makes it relatively easy to connect your web site to a database on your web or on a database server so that visitors can enter form data directly into your database. You can also enable visitors to access your database from a web page.

SEE ALSO

See "Importing Web Content" on page 20 for information on how to import a database or other file into your FrontPage web.

Create a Database Connection

1. Choose Web Settings from the Tools menu.

2. Click the Database tab.

3. Click Add.

4. Type a name for the database.

5. Select an option button that corresponds to the file location.

6. Click Browse, and then choose the type of file from the Files Of Type drop-down list box.

7. Select the database file, and then click OK.

8. Click OK.

9. Select the database, and click Verify to make sure the connection is working properly.

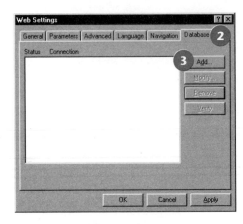

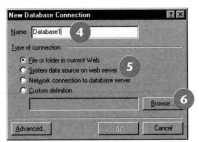

Sending Form Results to a Database

Once you have created a database connection with FrontPage, you can set up your forms to send their data directly to your database.

Send Form Results to a Database

1 Right-click the form whose data you want sent to a database.

2 Choose Form Properties from the shortcut menu.

3 Click the Send To Database option button.

4 Click Options.

5 Select the database in which you want to store the results.

6 Select the table in which you want to store the results.

7 Click the Saved Fields tab.

8 Select any Form fields that don't have a matching Database field, and click Modify.

9 Select a Database field, and then click OK.

10 Click OK again twice.

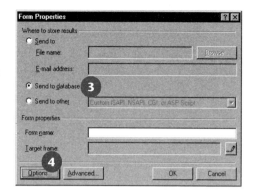

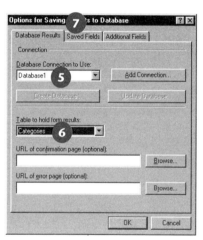

Inserting Database Results

Sometimes you'll find that you want to make data in your database directly accessible to your visitors, perhaps, for example, so they can search your inventory to see whether a certain product is in stock. FrontPage includes a special component that allows visitors to browse a database for certain fields you specify.

TIP

Limit returned records. *You can limit which records you want returned by clicking Advanced Options and then clicking Criteria. Click Add, and then select the field name, the type of comparison, and the value you want to query for.*

Use the Database Results Wizard

1. Create a new, blank web page in the web that contains your database.

2. Choose Database from the Insert menu and Results from the submenu.

3. Select the database connection you want to use from the drop-down list box.

4. Click Next.

5. Select a record source from the drop-down list box, and then click Next.

6. Optionally, use the Edit List and Move Options buttons to change what data you want returned and how you want it ordered.

7. Click Next.

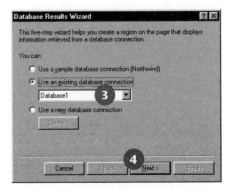

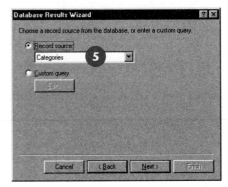

TIP

Publish your page. *To properly view a page with a database results component, publish the page to your web site and view it using your web browser.*

TIP

Save as .asp. *You have to save your web page as an Active Server Page. These pages work the same as HTML pages, except they contain content that is dependent on a server.*

8 Select Table or List from the drop-down list box to specify how you want to format returned records.

9 Select check boxes for the table or list options you want, and then click Next.

10 Click an option button to specify whether you want to split records into groups.

11 Click Finish.

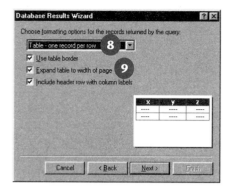

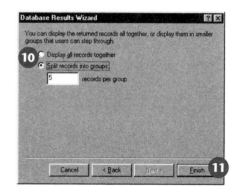

Administering a Web Site

The work of administering a large Internet web site often exceeds the burden that many web publishers will want to bear. Nevertheless, you should not assume that web site administration is out of reach or impractical if you are new to web publishing. Microsoft FrontPage provides numerous tools for making web site administration relatively easy for small web sites.

For example, you can make several changes to the web site's appearance and operation. You can easily change the number, type, and settings of the parameters that FrontPage's web wizards create and that the Substitution Components use. (A parameter is just a piece of information about a web site or web page that can be displayed by a Substitution Component.) You can also easily change or update the web site title and name.

Working with your web site's security is more involved, but it's still very straightforward to fine-tune your web site's security settings. For example, you can specify which users can browse, or visit, a web site. You can identify which users and groups of users can make changes to a web site's pages and images. And you can even specify which computers people can use to browse a web site.

Working with Parameters

FrontPage uses parameters to supply Substitution Components with commonly used pieces of information found in a web site, for example, your company name, e-mail address, and so forth. Although you typically create and set these configuration variables as part of running the wizard that creates a web site, you can make changes to the variables later.

SEE ALSO

See "Inserting Substitution Components" on page 140 for more information on using Substitution Components.

Add a Parameter

1. Choose Web Settings from the Tools menu.

2. Click the Parameters tab.

3. Click Add.

4. Type a name for the parameter in the Name text box.

5. Type the value for the parameter in the Value list box.

6. Click OK.

7. Click OK.

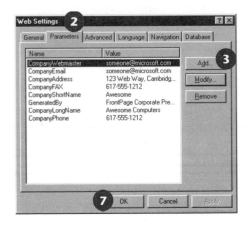

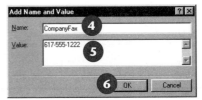

Change a Parameter

1. Choose Web Settings from the Tools menu.

2. Click the Parameters tab.

3. Select the configuration variable you want to change from the list box.

4. Click Modify.

5. Type the value for the parameter in the Value box.

6. Click OK.

7. Click OK.

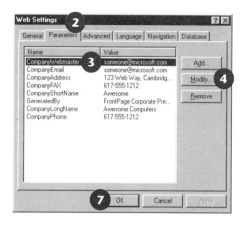

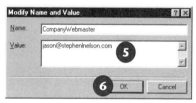

Changing Web Site Settings

When you create a web site, you give the web site a name that the web server as well as FrontPage will use to refer to the site. You also, indirectly, set the web site's language and choose the web site's characters. You can change these web site settings later by selecting Web Settings from the Tools menu.

TIP

Apply changes. *You can click Apply if you want to make a change using the Permissions dialog box—such as removing a user—without closing the dialog box.*

TIP

Valid filenames. *FrontPage will accept only filenames that do not include spaces or special characters other than the underscore (_) character.*

Change the Web Site Name

1. Choose Web Settings from the Tools menu.

2. Type the name for the web site in the Web Name text box.

3. Click OK.

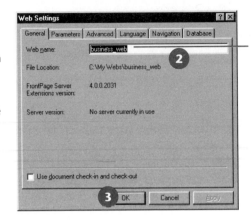

This is the name FrontPage uses for the directory holding the site's web pages and images.

Default Web Language. *The language you choose in the Default Web Language setting determines which language FrontPage Server Extensions uses to send messages to web site visitors when an error occurs or when additional user input is required.*

Change the Web Site's Language

1 Choose Web Settings from the Tools menu.

2 Click the Language tab.

3 Select the language you want the web site to use from the Server Message Language drop-down list box.

4 Select the default HTML coding style you want to use from the Default Page Encoding drop-down list box.

5 Click OK.

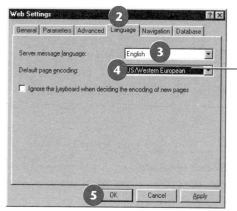

The Default Page Encoding selection you make determines which default character FrontPage will use for any new web pages you create.

10

Setting General Options

You can customize the way FrontPage works by using the Options command on the Tools menu. You can change how FrontPage starts, how it deals with out-of-date objects, and whether it warns you before applying Themes.

Set General Options

1 Choose Options from the Tools menu.

2 Select the first check box under Startup to change what FrontPage displays when it starts.

3 Select the second and third check boxes under Startup to check which programs are set as the default editor for Office documents and web pages.

4 Select the first check box under General to show the status bar.

5 Select the second and third check boxes under General to have FrontPage warn you when your components or your table of contents are out of date.

6 Select the fourth check box under General to have FrontPage warn you before permanently applying a theme.

7 Click OK.

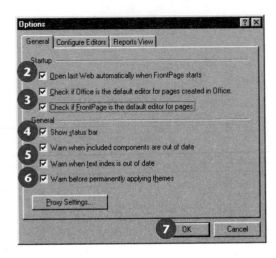

Options

General | Configure Editors | Reports View

Startup

2 ☑ Open last Web automatically when FrontPage starts

3 ☑ Check if Office is the default editor for pages created in Office.
☑ Check if FrontPage is the default editor for pages.

General

4 ☑ Show status bar

5 ☑ Warn when included components are out of date
☑ Warn when text index is out of date

6 ☑ Warn before permanently applying themes

Proxy Settings...

7 OK   Cancel

Configuring Editors

In the process of creating web pages, you work with a lot of different types of files: .html and .htm pages, .asp pages, .css style sheets, .jpg and .gif images, and so on. FrontPage lets you specify which program to use as your default editor for each type of file.

Add or Modify a File Type

1 Choose Options from the Tools menu.

2 Click the Configure Editors tab.

3 Select a file type from the list box, and click Add or Modify to create a new file type.

4 Type a three-letter file extension in the File Type text box, or modify the existing extension.

5 Type the name of the program you want to use in the Editor Name text box, or modify the existing name.

6 Click Browse to locate the program you want to use.

7 Click OK.

8 Click OK.

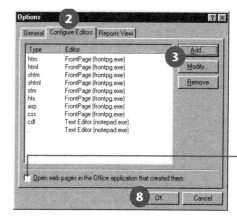

Select this check box to open web pages in the Office program that created them.

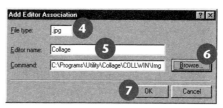

10

Changing Browser Options

The two major web browsers, Netscape Navigator and Microsoft Internet Explorer, display web pages somewhat differently, even in their newest versions. If visitors are viewing your site with older versions of these browsers, some features may not work at all. Fortunately, FrontPage lets you keep web pages compatible with older web browsers.

TIP

Set compatability for all pages. *To set the compatibility options for all pages in your web, choose Select All from the Edit menu while in the Folders view. Then change the compatibility options just as you would for a single page.*

Specify Compatibility Options

1. Choose Page Options from the Tools menu.

2. Click the Compatibility tab.

3. Select the type of Browser you want to be compatible with from the Browsers drop-down list box.

4. Select the oldest web browser you want to remain fully compatible with from the Browsers versions drop-down list box.

5. Select the type of web server your web site host is using.

6. Optionally, you can specify individual compatibility options by selecting the check boxes in the Technologies section.

7. Click OK.

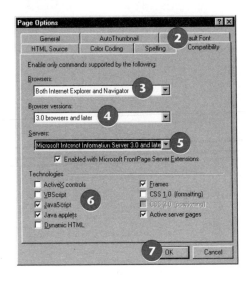

Working with Web Site Security

You can control access to your web site in a variety of ways. For example, you can specify who can make changes to the web site (such as adding or editing pages) and who can browse your web site. You can also specify which computers people can use to browse your web site.

TIP

Root web permissions. *If the current web is the root web on the server, the Permissions dialog box does not have a Settings tab. The web already has unique permissions.*

TIP

No permissions allowed. *Some web servers do not allow you to set user permissions.*

Use Unique Permissions for a Web Site

1 Choose Security from the Tools menu and Permissions from the submenu.

2 Click the Use Unique Permissions For This Web option button.

3 Click OK.

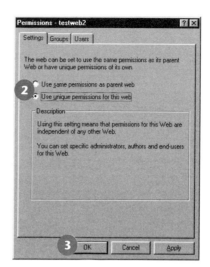

Adding and Removing Users

After you have specified that you want to use unique permissions for web site users, you need to build a list of users and designate the permissions for each user. You might, on occasion, also want to remove users from the list to deny them access to browse the web site.

TIP

Administrators only.
To change the web site permissions, you must have administrator rights.

TIP

Add a user. *To specify a new user for a web site, you must first indicate that you want to use a unique set of permissions for the web site.*

Specify a New User for a Web Site

1. Choose Security from the Tools menu and Permissions from the submenu.

2. Click the Users tab.

3. Click Add.

4. Select the domain from the Obtain List From drop-down list box.

5. Select the new user's name from the Names list box.

6. Click Add.

7. Select an option under Allow Users To to specify what this user can do.

8. Click OK.

9. Click OK.

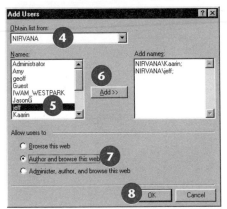

Remove a User from a Web Site

1. Choose Security from the Tools menu and Permissions from the submenu.

2. Click the Users tab.

3. Select a user name from the list box.

4. Click Remove.

5. Click OK.

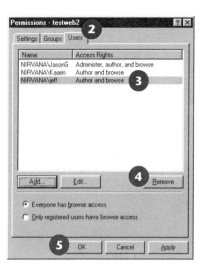

10

Specifying User Permissions

Once you have specified unique permissions for a web site, you can grant permissions for each individual user. You can give users varying levels of permission—from the ability to browse the web site only to the ability to author and administer the web site.

TIP

Set permissions first. *To specify who can browse a web site, you must first indicate that you want to use a unique set of permissions for the web site. You must also do this to change an existing user's permissions.*

Specify Who Can Browse a Web Site

1. Choose Security from the Tools menu and Permissions from the submenu.

2. Click the Users tab.

3. Click an option button to specify who can and who can't browse this web site.

4. Click OK.

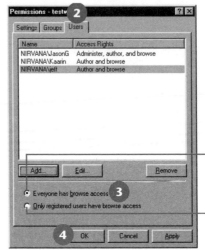

Select this option if you want everyone to be able to browse the web site.

Select this option if you want only registered users to be able to browse the web site.

About permission types.
Browsing permission gives the user the right to view the web site but not make any changes. Authoring permission gives the user the right to create, edit, and delete web pages in a web site. Administering permission gives the user the right to set permissions and passwords for the web site and create new web sites within the current web.

Change an Existing User's Permissions for a Web Site

1 Choose Security from the Tools menu and Permissions from the submenu.

2 Click the Users tab.

3 Select a user name from the list box.

4 Click Edit.

5 Click an option button under Allow User To to specify what this user can do.

6 Click OK.

7 Click OK.

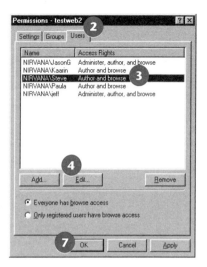

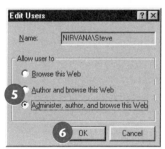

10

Adding and Removing User Groups

As with specifying individual user permissions for a web site, you can also specify permissions for a group of users. You do this by building a list of users to which you grant some level of access permission to the web site, and then you specify the level of permission for each group.

TIP

Set permissions first. *To remove a group from a web site, you must first indicate that you want to use a unique set of permissions for the web site.*

Specify a New User Group for a Web Site

1 Choose Security from the Tools menu and Permissions from the submenu.

2 Click the Groups tab.

3 Click Add.

4 Select the group from the Names list box.

5 Click Add.

6 Click OK.

7 Click OK.

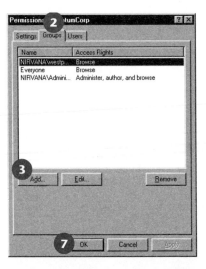

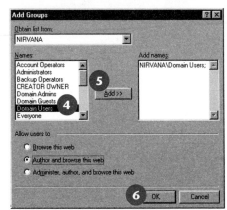

Remove a User Group from a Web Site

1. Choose Security from the Tools menu and Permissions from the submenu.

2. Click the Groups tab.

3. Select a group from the list box.

4. Click Remove.

5. Click OK.

10

Changing Group Permissions

After you have compiled a list of user groups that you want to grant permission to browse your web site and have designated specific permissions for each group, you may at some point want to change a group's permission. Luckily, this is very easy to do.

Change an Existing User Group's Permissions

1 Choose Security from the Tools menu.

2 Click the Groups tab.

3 Select a group from the list box.

4 Click Edit.

5 Click an option button under Allow User To to specify what the users in this group can do.

6 Click OK.

7 Click OK.

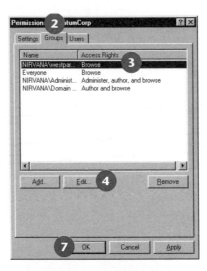

Deleting a Web Site

If you create a web site that you no longer use—perhaps the web site was a practice site that you used to learn FrontPage, for example— you can and should delete the web site. (You do this because web sites, particularly those that use many images, require voluminous quantities of disk space.)

TIP

No Undo. *You can't undelete a web site using the Microsoft Windows 98 or Windows NT Recycle Bin. For this reason, you'll want to make sure you really do want to delete a web site before choosing the Delete FrontPage Web command.*

Delete a Web Site

1 Open the web site you want to delete.

2 Right-click the root directory, or highest-level folder, in the Folder List.

3 Choose Delete from the shortcut menu

4 Select whether you want to remove all FrontPage information from the folder, leaving data intact, or whether you want to delete the web entirely.

5 Click OK.

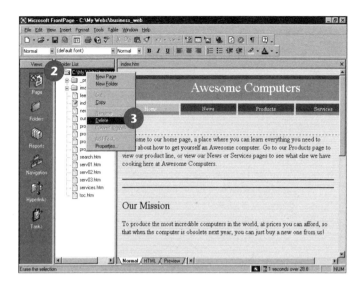

10

Checking Files In and Out

Working on the development of a web site with other people presents some challenges; one of the biggest is preventing one person from inadvertently overwriting another person's changes. FrontPage 2000 helps alleviate this problem by allowing users to check out pages, so the only person who can edit the page is the person who checked it out. After editing the page, the user then checks it back in.

Enable Document Check-In and Check-Out

1 Choose Web Settings from the Tools menu.

2 Select the Use Document Check-In and Check-Out check box.

3 Click OK.

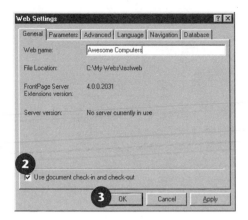

Check Out a File

1 Right-click a file in the Folder List.

2 Choose Check Out from the shortcut menu.

3 Click Yes in the dialog box to open and check out the file. To open the file without checking it out, click No.

A lock means the file is checked out.

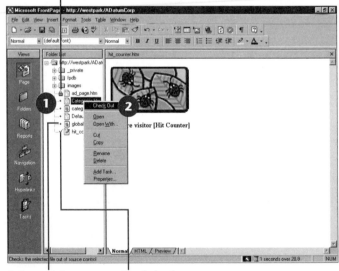

A green dot means the file is checked in.

A red check means you have the file checked out.

Check out files. *Although FrontPage allows you to edit a web page you haven't checked out, you could overwrite someone's edits when you save or publish the file. Always check out files you're going to edit to prevent you or someone else from losing changes.*

Check In a File

1 Right-click a checked-out file in the Folder List.

2 Choose Check-In from the shortcut menu.

Specifying Pages Not to Publish

FrontPage lets you mark certain files that you don't want to publish to your web site. You can use this feature to keep new pages off the web site until they are finished or to keep special files stored locally.

TIP

Publish an excluded file. *To publish a file you've excluded from publishing, clear the Exclude This File When Publishing The Rest Of The Web check box.*

Specify a Page Not to Publish

1. Right-click the file you want to exclude from publishing in the Folder list.

2. Choose Properties from the shortcut menu.

3. Click the Workgroup tab.

4. Select the Exclude This File When Publishing The Rest Of The Web check box.

5. Click OK.

Using Add-Ins

FrontPage 2000 provides support for third-party add-ins, or plug-in programs, to enhance the features of FrontPage.

Use the Accessibility Add-In

1 Choose Add-Ins from the Tools menu.

2 Click Add to locate the add-in.

3 Select the add-in.

4 Click OK.

5 Click OK to load the add-in.

Index

The manuscript for this book was prepared and submitted to Microsoft Press in electronic form. Text files were prepared using Microsoft Word 97. Pages were composed by Stephen L. Nelson, Inc., using PageMaker for Windows, with text in Stone Sans and display type in Stone Serif and Stone Serif Semibold. Composed pages were delivered to the printer as electronic prepress files.

Cover Designer
Tim Girvin Design

Graphic Layout
Stefan Knorr

Indexer
Julie Kawabata

Stay in the running for maximum productivity.

These are *the* answer books for business users of Microsoft® Office 2000. They are packed with everything from quick, clear instructions for new users to comprehensive answers for power users—the authoritative reference to keep by your computer and use every day. THE RUNNING SERIES—learning solutions made by Microsoft.

- RUNNING MICROSOFT EXCEL 2000
- RUNNING MICROSOFT OFFICE 2000 PREMIUM
- RUNNING MICROSOFT OFFICE 2000 PROFESSIONAL
- RUNNING MICROSOFT OFFICE 2000 SMALL BUSINESS
- RUNNING MICROSOFT WORD 2000
- RUNNING MICROSOFT POWERPOINT® 2000
- RUNNING MICROSOFT ACCESS 2000
- RUNNING MICROSOFT INTERNET EXPLORER 5
- RUNNING MICROSOFT FRONTPAGE® 2000
- RUNNING MICROSOFT OUTLOOK® 2000

Microsoft®

mspress.microsoft.com

Register Today!

Return this
Microsoft® FrontPage® 2000 At a Glance
registration card today

Microsoft®Press
mspress.microsoft.com

1-57231-951-8

Microsoft® FrontPage® 2000 At a Glance

_____ _____ _____
FIRST NAME   MIDDLE INITIAL   LAST NAME

_____
INSTITUTION OR COMPANY NAME

_____
ADDRESS

_____

_____ _____ _____
CITY   STATE   ZIP

                                                          (   ) _____
_____
E-MAIL ADDRESS   PHONE NUMBER

U.S. and Canada addresses only. Fill in information above and mail postage-free.
Please mail only the bottom half of this page.

*For information about Microsoft Press®
products, visit our Web site at*
mspress.microsoft.com

Microsoft®*Press*

BUSINESS REPLY MAIL
FIRST-CLASS MAIL   PERMIT NO. 108   REDMOND WA

POSTAGE WILL BE PAID BY ADDRESSEE

NO POSTAGE
NECESSARY
IF MAILED
IN THE
UNITED STATES

MICROSOFT PRESS
PO BOX 97017
REDMOND, WA 98073-9830